Catherine Doherty

SERVANT *of* GOD

The significance of her life for the Church,
and the present state of her cause for canonization.

Robert Wild

MADONNA HOUSE PUBLICATIONS
Combermere, Ontario, Canada

Madonna House Publications
2888 Dafoe Rd
Combermere ON K0J 1L0

www.madonnahouse.org/publications

Catherine Doherty: Servant of God by Fr. Robert Wild.
© 2005 Madonna House Publications. All rights reserved.

First printing, September 29, 2005 — feast of the Archangels

Printed in Canada

Design by Rob Huston

Library and Archives Canada Cataloguing in Publication

Wild, Robert
  Catherine Doherty : servant of God / Robert Wild.

ISBN 0-921440-95-2

  1. Doherty, Catherine de Hueck, 1896–1985. 2. Catholics—
Canada—Biography. 3. Social reformers—Canada—Biography.
4. Madonna House Apostolate. I. Title.

BX4705.D56W555 2005   282'.092   C2005-906011-5

PART ONE

CATHERINE DOHERTY AND MADONNA HOUSE

....

Howl my soul, howl.
Cry to the Lord for his Church.
Howl my soul, howl.
For the Church is in pain.
Look, she lies in the dust of a thousand roads.
No one stops; the Good Samaritan is not seen
At the bend of those roads yet!

If this were the only quote one read from the writings of Catherine Doherty, the reader would think she was a raving reactionary with a distorted view of all the good things that have happened in the Church since the Second Vatican Council. However, as with anyone's writings, each statement must be seen as parts of the whole. Catherine had a very clear view of both the beauty and sins of the Church. I quote this fragment, not so much to emphasize her vision of the wounds of the Church, as to communicate something of her *passionate love for the Church.* For the purposes of this brief introduction to her life, I will focus on her love and concern for the Church as central to what the Holy Spirit was doing through her. He was inspiring her to create a new model of the Church in the community she founded. The Church now calls them "ecclesial communities."

Who Was Catherine Doherty?

She was one of the estimated 5 million Russian refugees fleeing from the revolution. She had an extraordinary awareness of Christ suffering in the poor of the world. She set out to console him, wash his feet, and dry his tears, first in the poor of Toronto, then of Harlem, then of the thousands who would come to the Christian center she founded in Ontario, Canada—Madonna House. This is a brief account of her life and how the community she founded continues to incarnate her charisms, and to be an expression of the Church in this time of history.

A Personal Note

May I share a personal experience as part of this introduction? I do so because the inspiration which led me to join Madonna House is probably similar to the inspiration which has led thousands of people to join the new ecclesial movements and communities, namely, a desire for a deeper and more living experience of the Church.

Before I came to Madonna House in 1971 I had had several years of monastic experience where I lived in a total Christian environment. There I met some very holy abbots and monks. Later, as a parish priest, I was involved in the charismatic renewal, the Cursillo, and other movements of the 60s. As I look back I see that I had really been seeking, in all these movements, a new expression of the Church that I had been reading about in the Council documents. Where was this Church spoken of so glowingly by the Council Fathers?

When I encountered Combermere and Catherine I recognized, due to my monastic experience, that she was a religious genius, and that she had accomplished the magnificent achievement of putting together a totally Christian environment as I had experienced in the monasteries. It was different, of course. Madonna House was/is a kind of lay monasticism. But the deep monastic, traditional elements were still there—poverty, obedience, chastity, simplicity, prayer, manual work, silence, and community life—but they were all harmonized in a different *lay mode*, you might say. (Were not most of early monastics lay people?)

Secondly, due to my searchings as a parish priest, I recognized that Madonna House was a new, living, model of the Church which Vatican II had articulated. In the 1950s, five priests had already joined Madonna House. They had been reading earlier Church documents in which the Popes were calling for Catholic action. These priests saw the need to encourage the lay apostolates. They, too, were seeking a new, more vibrant expression of the Church. One of them, Fr. Émile Marie Brière, visited a certain Fr. Fulton Sheen in 1944, who said that the Church at that time was not on the offensive or the defensive but on the *expository*, that is, seeking to express who she really was. How perceptive his insight was has been vindicated by the Church's own reflection on these movements at the end of the last century. (More of that below.)

And there was something else about Catherine that I didn't realize for many years but had subconsciously experienced in my monastic formation. It was the fact that I had received the Catholic spiritual and ascetical tradition *through holy men who were living it themselves*. Very few people now have the opportunity to receive our tradition in this way. They receive it, if at all, through books, class work, a good Christian family, a holy friend. Few have the opportunity to be immersed in a totally Catholic environment for a few years and to be taught by elders who have received the tradition, and are passing it on through their own living witness. I don't know if a great tradition can really be passed on in any other way.

What I saw in Catherine, in Combermere, was that people were experiencing the great traditions of East and West through the life and teaching of a very alive, dynamic, charismatic, Christian genius. It wasn't exactly old Russia she was transmitting; it wasn't exactly the Western tradition either: it was both, in some unique expression.

Theological Framework

One way to present a saintly person's life and vocation is to make a historical list of facts and dates, like in an encyclopedia. This can convey a lot of information about the person but may fail to communicate the person's inner life and his or her significance for the Church.

Another approach, which I will adopt here, is more incarnational and holistic: It is to try and show how grace came in and through a person's life journey. It may not cover all the biographical details, but it can sufficiently outline the main events which forged the person's character, mission and holiness.

It would also be helpful to try and demonstrate how the graces a person received gradually took on flesh and blood in apostolic endeavors, and in the lives of those who were influenced by him or her.

A still further desirable dimension would be to show how a person's life was part of a wider movement of the Holy Spirit. It is through such an incarnational and holistic approach that I will attempt to briefly present the life of Catherine Kolyschkine de Hueck Doherty (1896–1985). I will try to show how Madonna House, the community she founded, exemplifies her charism, and what significance her legacy has for the Church.

Ecclesial Communities

There are two recent books which offer a penetrating understanding of the new movements and communities in the Church. When I read them I was amazed at how accurately they described Madonna House, which had been in existence long before this reflection on the ecclesial communities began. (We are one of the oldest of these new communities.)

The first is entitled *Movements in the Church*. It contains the proceedings of the World Congress of Ecclesial

Movements convened in May, 1998, in Rome, by the Council for the Laity. The second is *The Ecclesial Movements in the Pastoral Concern of the Bishops.* It contains the proceedings of a seminar held in Rome June 16-18, 1999, again promoted by the Council for the Laity. In using citations from these books I will simply refer to the numbers #2 and #4 respectively, their publication numbers in a series of books. (Available from: Pontifical Council for the Laity, Palazzo San Calisto, 00120 Vatican City).

Theology of the Ecclesial Communities

I begin with the Church's own mature assessment of the 20th century lay "movement of communities" because it highlights an inspiration of the Holy Spirit which unifies one of the main directions and purposes of Catherine's life.

Pope John Paul II saw the new ecclesial movements and communities as the providential response of the Holy Spirit to fulfill the great need for mature Christian personalities and communities at the end of the millennium. Some of the lay apostolic ventures of the last century—but not all—evolved into these ecclesial realities. In addressing the above-mentioned *World Congress of the Ecclesial Movements* in Rome, May, 1998, he said:

> What is meant today by 'movement'? The term is often used to refer to realities that differ among themselves, sometimes even by reason of their canonical structure. Though that term certainly cannot exhaust or capture the wealth of forms aroused by the life-giving creativity of the Spirit of Christ, it does indicate a concrete ecclesial reality with predominately lay membership, a journey of faith and a Christian witness which bases its own pedagogical method on a precise charism given to the person of the founder in specific circumstances and ways. #2/18

Madonna House is one of these new "concrete ecclesial realities" which the Pope is describing.

Ten years earlier, in *Christifideles Laici* (1988), the Magna Charta of the laity, the Pope spoke about these new ecclesial realities in this way:

> In recent days the phenomenon of lay people associating among themselves has taken on a character of particular variety and vitality. In some ways lay associations have always been present throughout the Church's history as various confraternities, third orders and sodalities testify even today. However in modern times such lay groups have received a special stimulus, resulting in the birth and spread of a multiplicity of group forms: associations, groups, communities, movements. We can speak of a new era of group endeavors of the lay faithful. (No.29)

Many communities in the history of the Church started out as "lay," and the persons who founded them were "lay." Only later did some of the founders become "religious," and their communities "Orders." Had the Church not recognized, in our times, that the Spirit was doing something new, many of these lay groups might have taken this "religious" path of development. Their new characteristics might have been clipped and molded to make them "fit" older canonical forms. However, beginning with Pius XII's *Provida Mater Ecclesia* (1947), which dealt with lay people taking promises in Secular Institutes, these new ecclesial realities were coming to birth through the Holy Spirit's guidance.

The Charism of a Foundress

A theology of founders and foundresses has arisen since Vatican II. I will simply state that Catherine saw herself as having been called by the Lord to be the foundress of, first, Friendship House, and then Madonna House (both of which we shall be considering). Her awareness of being a foundress grew over a period of time, as it often did with other founders and foundresses. In the early 1940s she begins referring to herself as the foundress of Friendship House; in 1970, after almost 30 years in the service of the Lord, she began writing a series of letters to the community of Madonna House entitled, "Letters From the Foundress." Shortly afterwards she wrote a Constitution, or Way of Life. In her voluminous writings she has given Madonna House its spirit and direction. She certainly believed that the Lord had called her to found a new family in the Church.

When the Lord desires to create a new community, he speaks to someone. This brief presentation of the life of Catherine and Madonna House will center on the theological reality of *the charism of a foundress.* Charism simply means "gift." The Holy Spirit orders and enriches the whole Church by his gifts and graces (*Lumen Gentium*, 12). He himself is *the Gift* of the New Testament. By his coming at Pentecost he gave birth to the whole Church; by his continual coming he nourishes and distributes gifts to all its members.

A number of charisms are listed in the New Testament (1 Cor. 12); but there are many others. Of particular interest for our purposes is what Pope Paul VI, in *Evangelica Testificatio*, called "the charisms of your founders whom God has raised up in his Church" (11) . (Vatican II simply spoke of the *spirit* of founders and foundresses.)

Sometimes attempts are made to pinpoint one special gift of such people in order to distinguish them from other founders and foundresses: "What is the charism of St. Francis which distinguishes him from St. Dominic?" Such questions and distinctions have a certain validity. However, concentrating on one particular aspect of a founder can obscure the fact that what we are really dealing with is a *charismatic person.* At the very end of his valuable study, *Foundresses, Founders, and Their Religious Families,*[1] Fr. John Lozano states what I wish to make my overall approach to presenting the charismatic dimension in Catherine's life:

> We must face the fact that the charism, properly speaking, cannot be defined. Rather, it must be described by gathering up those traits through which it gradually appeared in those who first lived it, as well as in the successive generations who received it. It is not something that can be expressed in a few words. For if it were reduced to just a few words, many of its really different manifestations in history would seem to blur and coincide. (92)

The following may be broadening the concept of charism somewhat. However, seeing Catherine, or any founder or foundress as a *charismatic person*, and understanding "charism" as a many-faceted reality instead of a single specific grace, is more accurate and helpful. You might say that the charism of Catherine is *Catherine herself*.

I recall, in this context, the best imaginative definition of a saint I ever read, given, of course, by a child: "A saint is somebody in a stained glass window, and light comes through every part of him." Light comes through *the whole person*, not just one aspect of him or her.

Generally speaking, the Holy Spirit gives graces to these outstanding people *in and through their history*:

> We must never forget that divine grace is always given to real living persons with their own individual temperament and qualities, yet formed through a series of experiences and conditioned by the environment in which they lived. Not only the temperament and character of a person, but also time and society have a deep influence on the religious experience of the saints. (Ibid., 76)

Trying to see how the Holy Spirit communicated graces to founders in and through their history, character, and upbringing, is a more accurate way of understanding who they were.

Another essential aspect of my presentation will be what Pope John Paul II, in the above cited address to the movements in St. Peter's Square, called *the communicative dimension of the charism*:

> By their nature, charisms are communicative and give rise to that 'spiritual affinity among persons' and to that friendship in Christ which is the origin of 'movements.' The passage from the original charism to the movement happens through the mysterious attraction that the founder holds for all those who become involved in his spiritual experience. In this way movements officially recognized by ecclesiastical authority offer themselves as forms of self-fulfillment and as facets of the one Church. (#2, 222)

Catherine's life spanned almost a whole century. It would not be possible, in so short a treatment, to do justice to her entire life.[2] I will be concentrating, therefore, on those aspects of Catherine's life which were particularly destined by the Holy Spirit to be ingredients in the ecclesial community she founded. All her teaching can be seen as guiding people to authentic "self-fulfillment," that is, authentic holiness, in order to form the community into a true "facet of the one Church."

To Restore All Things in Christ

If people are attracted to a certain Order or community it is usually because there is some kind of spiritual resonance, "spiritual affinity," in their hearts with the founder/foundress of that particular community. The charisms of the founder can be and are, in some degree, communicated to the members through the Holy Spirit. It is this particular charism, inspired by the Holy Spirit, which binds them together in a specific way.

I emphasized that a charism cannot be defined in one word. But if I were asked if Catherine's charism *could* be summed up in one word or phrase, I would say it was centered in the motto she chose for the community from Pope Pius X's first encyclical: "To Restore All Things In Christ."

In the early years of her apostolate she tried to accomplish this restoration through the spiritual and corporal works of mercy; and especially through her efforts for interracial justice. As we shall see, it was during the third and final phase of her life—Madonna House—that she began to incarnate this charism of restoration in as many ways as possible. She sought to create, in miniature, a world where all things really were restored in Christ. Bishop Albert-Marie de Monleon, O.P., entitled his talk on the new movements, "Places of a Transfigured Humanity." (#2,149 ff.) She believed that the sparks emanating from such a community could help to ignite the Church and the whole world.

While I will be trying to describe how Madonna House is *presently* seeking to live out Catherine's vision, I would emphasize that we are only at an early stage of our growth. Her vision is as comprehensive as the Church itself, since it is the Spirit's intention in these communities to express the very nature of the Church. Catherine's charism to restore all things in Christ is really unlimited in its scope. Any form of the apostolate is open to us. Presently we are involved in certain expressions. My point is that the various aspects of her charismatic life could be expressed in different ways in the future.

One of the main reasons for this "open future" is that the charisms of a founder or foundress cannot be identified with their external works. The charism exists in the interior grace which inspired their activities. These activities can change, and probably ought to. (As the philosophers tell us, for something to remain the same, it has to change.)

Not everything in her life is equally essential for, or able to be communicated to, the community's identity and mission. Some graces are personal to her. (For example, her sufferings and her degree of sanctity.) In order to present a harmonious picture of her life and that of Madonna House, I will, in each section, mention certain graces of Catherine's life, seeking to show 1) something of the historical context through which she received them, and 2) how these graces/charisms are presently manifested in Madonna House. In this way we can achieve this more holistic understanding of her life and community. It is the Holy Spirit who gives birth to new communities in the Church. Catherine loved to call the Holy Spirit, in her Russian fashion, "the Crimson Dove."

"I Am Russian"

Although Catherine, ethnically speaking, was only one-quarter Russian, she had a Russian mind and heart. People whose ancestors originally came from Western Europe, and who had lived in Russia for centuries, became russified. On one occasion, towards the end of her life, Catherine expressed to a friend that, although she had tried to conform, to some extent, to Western ways of thinking and acting, she was never able to really do it. "I am Russian," she said, "and I always will be." Her Russianess will be important to remember as we look at her life and try to understand who she was.

For those of us who knew her, it took many years before we were able to re-focus our Western minds and hearts and see her life, attitudes, and speech with something of an Eastern mentality. Russians, and Easterners generally, easily understand her; we Westerners have to really work at it. We are literal-minded, logical. Her thinking was more poetical, "iconographic," you might say.

Where she often used images, and therefore was speaking figuratively, we would tend to take her words literally.

This difference came home to me recently as I was reading some sophisticated, theological critique of her writings, which took every one of her words very literally. I think, generally, the author missed the point of her particular grace. She wasn't always theologically precise! Tolkien once said that truth is best communicated through symbols—imaginatively. She was a genius at that. She painted word-pictures. When someone once quoted her own words to her to win an argument, she said: "I will not be bound by my own words!" I simply emphasize that she was Russian, a woman, a poet, not a trained theologian, but someone taught by God. I make a plea that we try to understand her teaching in that light.

A Woman of the Century

The details of Catherine's birth in Nijni Novgorod, Russia, in 1896, are less important for our specific purposes than the fact that, falling asleep in the Lord in 1985, her life spanned almost the whole of the 20th century. The Holy Spirit used most of the cataclysmic events of that century to mold her character and to communicate graces to her in order to enrich the community and the whole Church. Speaking for myself, I can't imagine going through the suffering that she experienced. Dostoevsky, her countryman and favorite Russian author, said that without suffering we will never know many truths about life. She knew most of them.

If we just think for a moment of some of these events in which she was personally involved, we can get an idea, however inadequate, of the scope of her experience, the sufferings she endured, the challenges to her faith, and the greatness of her following of Christ.

She experienced the First World War, the Russian Revolution, the Great Depression in North America, the

Second World War, the racial integration movement in the United States, the Second Vatican Council and its aftermath. She did not simply read about these events: she was part of them. It is because she came through all them with her faith flaming and her love stronger than ever that she can serve as a safe guide for others in the life of faith. She serves for mine.

The testing of her faith was not limited to one convent or monastery, to one small geographical area, or to one homogeneous group of people. As a wife and mother, writer and lecturer, as one whose experience and gifts could form a whole community of men and women, she was a kind of total person, involved with life on many levels.

Although the members of Madonna House do not, of course, have her experiences of all of these events, she has bequeathed to us her faith responses to them. Part of our heritage is the wisdom God taught her through a long and difficult human life. The depth of her spiritual legacy stems both from her personal gifts and the extraordinary range of experiences which finely honed and forged them.

C.S. Lewis said that life is iconoclastic, shattering all our theoretical ideas about it. The extraordinary range of her experiences not only shattered any pre-conceived notions she might have had about life. They also led her to a deep wisdom that came not from books but from this shattering. Her own actual, living presence could also be quite iconoclastic for others! The intensity of her union with God could shatter the mediocrity and pretensions of those who encountered her. Although many people only met or heard her speak on one occasion, still, their lives were often changed by that single powerful and charismatic encounter.

Family Background

Her father, Theodore Kolyschkine, was born in the Russian-occupied section of Poland in the mid-19th century of a Russian father, who was stationed there, and a Polish, Roman Catholic mother. It is possible that her father was secretly baptized as a Catholic. (There is a family story that the mother asked that her first child be baptized a Catholic. Having a Russian father, it would have been illegal for Theodore to have been baptized publicly as a Catholic.) Thus Catherine's own breathing with the two lungs of Catholicism and Orthodoxy (a favorite expression of Pope John Paul II) began already in her father's loins.

Her mother, Emma Thompson, was of purely European descent, her ancestors being part of that professional class whom Peter the Great invited to westernize Russia. But although Emma was Western European, her deep soul also had been "russified."

Catherine was baptized into the Russian Orthodox Church. She probably did not have much of a formal, literate education in Orthodoxy as we would understand "religious instruction" in the West. What she did receive was a formation in the Orthodox sense: the experience of the liturgy, home customs, pilgrimages, and service to the poor.

My Russian Yesterdays

Catherine related many of these experiences in her book, *My Russian Yesterdays*.[3] It gives some idea of how she was formed. It graphically describes the sacral world of her origins that would one day contrast so sharply with the West into which the Revolution would expel her. If we had some appreciation of the clash within her between the almost medieval world from which she came and the secularized West, we would have an experiential understanding of the origin of the inner drive she experienced to "restore all things in Christ."

Besides chapters on Herbs, Education, Sports, and almost every area of life, Catherine has several chapters on the religious aspects of her upbringing. As an example, she relates the splendor of the Easter liturgy she experienced as a young child:

> In a loud, penetrating voice, the priest proclaimed, 'Christ is risen! Christ is risen!' The whole congregation answered, 'Truly He is risen!' Then the priest kissed the deacon, who then passed the kiss of peace down the clerical line.
>
> At this point a Westerner would have been sorely puzzled, for everyone in the church turned around and kissed his neighbor, exchanging over and over again the joyous salutation of the priest: 'Christ is risen! Truly he is risen!'
>
> At that moment all the church bells started ringing freely, with a song of great gladness, as if repeating, 'Yes, Christ is risen!' Beautiful and unforgettable was the sound of the 'forty times forty' bells of Moscow. (64)

She remembers carrying the Easter fire home through the darkness. She recalls the long pilgrimages to the holy monasteries. In another of her books, *Not Without Parables*, she re-tells—adding her own imaginative flavor!—the miraculous stories she heard while sitting at the feet of the holy pilgrims who were given hospitality in her home.

Her mother was "quite ecumenical." She always put "Lutheran" on her passport, but her son Andre told me that when they lived in Brussels after the War they would attend a variety of churches. She probably did not have too many strict dogmatic opinions! Her faith was lived, expressed mostly in her extraordinary love for the poor, in teaching Catherine about the dignity of all work and of all men and women.

One of the expressions of the "Catholic lung" of her father was manifested in the fact that when the family moved, due to his business, to Alexandria, Egypt, Catherine was put into a Roman Catholic school run by the Sisters of Sion. (This Order had been founded to promote unity between the people of Israel and Christianity.) A strict Slavophil Russian would hardly have placed his impressionable young Orthodox child in a Catholic school. Here Catherine was certainly exposed to the Mass, instruction in the Catholic faith, and the full panoply of Catholic devotions. Some of the Lord's most fundamental graces to her were implanted during that time.

For example, as a young child in that school she was so moved by the sufferings of Christ on the Cross that she went around to all the crucifixes and tried to take him off. The antics of a child? Yes, but this action revealed that, very early, the Spirit had implanted in her a profound desire to assuage the sufferings of Christ, to console him in his pain and loneliness, to take him off his cross, to wipe his face like Veronica. This passion to console Jesus became *the absolute center of Catherine's spirituality*, and it was born in her childlike heart in this Catholic school in Alexandria.

During the summer Catherine's family often went to visit her Catholic grandmother in Poland. She said she learned a great deal about Catholicism from her. The following quote from the introduction to her book, *My Russian Yesterdays*, reveals the religious world in which Catherine grew up, the geographical matrix of her Orthodox/Catholic spirit, the seedbed of her longing for the reunion of East and West:

The customs, celebrations, prayers, and the 'ways of doing things' that you will find in these pages were common to both Catholic and Orthodox in Russia. In those days, parts of Poland, Lithuania, and a great part of Catholic Ukraine officially formed part and parcel of 'Russia.' Unofficially, intermarriage, the close living together of neighbors, the influx of Russians into the Catholic parts of the country and vice versa—all had their effects. I give them to you as they came to me, from living with my grandmother's folks near Warsaw, and with my grandfather's near Moscow. (v-vi)

We, the members of Madonna House, speculate among ourselves as to why Catherine, when she came to England after escaping from Russia, made a profession of faith in the Catholic Church. (Her name is in the records of converts in the Westminster archives). We know where and when it happened (London, November 29, 1919), but the "why" remains somewhat shrouded in mystery. In London she had come across a convent of those very Sisters of Sion who had taught her in Alexandria. She received instructions and entered the Church. But why? Several reasons come to mind.

She had been raised in the two worlds of Catholicism and Orthodoxy, as the above quote testifies. As a young girl, not over-educated in doctrinal matters, she might not really have seen all that much creedal difference between Catholicism and Orthodoxy. Also, her father used to read to them, as children, from the works of Vladimir Soloviev. Considered by many to be the greatest Russian philosopher/theologian, he himself made a public confession of faith in the Pope as the "wonder-working icon of Christian unity," and this in the 1880s in Russia. Soloviev taught that Christ could not really be divided. She was undoubtedly influenced by him. (His picture has a very prominent place in the main house in Combermere.)

Believing that she would never be able to return to Russia, perhaps there was an impelling sense to identify, now, with the new world in which she was going to live. No form of Protestantism would have appealed to her, and Catholicism was already in her bones.

Privately, she retained some of her Orthodox customs all her life: icons, bowing before the Blessed Sacrament instead of genuflecting, prostrations at times, perhaps even a preference for the Orthodox liturgy. However, in her outward life and her teaching of others, she would have appeared and acted pretty much as a Roman Catholic.

In her diaries, for example, until the 1960s, there is very little indication of her Orthodox spirituality. At that time Fr. Joseph Raya, a Melchite (Eastern Greek Catholic) priest, became associated with the community. One day he and one of his parishioners walked into the dining room carrying two huge icons as gifts for the community. Something happened in Catherine's heart. All the memories of Holy Russia flooded back into her. It seemed the time had arrived for her to now draw as well upon her Orthodox roots for the enriching of Madonna House and the Church.

From this time onwards—the last 25 years of her life—she began writing her Russian books: *Poustinia, Sobornost, Strannik, Molchanie, Urodivoi*. They are not exactly Orthodox, or Western, spirituality: they are an interweaving of both. Since her arrival in the West she had tried personally to assimilate, into her heart, Western Catholicism. These later books now expressed the flowing together of the two streams of East and West that had begun mingling in her heart in her mother's womb, and that had been fusing in a hidden manner during her whole life. This legacy is an essential part of the Madonna House apostolate.

The Two Lungs of Madonna House

If you came to our main center in Combermere, Ontario, Canada, or to any one of our smaller houses, and knew nothing about us, for the first few hours you might wonder whether we were Catholic or Orthodox. (In fact, sometimes people ask us that very question.) Our houses, and our chapels, display icons as well as statues. This is fairly common today, but it was not so common 40 years ago. And when they hear that our foundress was Russian, and when they see the many Eastern books on our shelves, well, they wonder.

Catherine wanted us to understand Orthodoxy, the great Christian tradition of the East. However, she definitely wanted us to be Catholic. In fact, there was a long period where she was fearful that we would not understand Orthodoxy; then a period when she feared that we would "go too far" in Eastern ways. But long before Pope John Paul II articulated his famous "two lungs" phrase, Catherine had been led by the Spirit to integrate, in our community, the two great traditions. She saw this as part of her mission, and it is part of the apostolate of Madonna House.

Fr. Raya became Archbishop Raya, and eventually a full-time member of Madonna House. (Another indication of the different states of life drawn into ecclesial communities.) He retired in Combermere, and for many years celebrated Byzantine liturgies, as well as teaching us about the spirit of the Eastern Church. We strive for unity between East and West by our prayer, by trying to understand Orthodoxy ourselves, and by helping others to understand it. We are not presently involved in any projects or programs to attain this unity. It is by seeking to integrate Orthodoxy into our hearts and lives that we hope to be a small bridge of unity in the Church.

"Going Into the People"

In the latter part of the 19th century, and the early part of the 20th, Emma, Catherine's mother, was involved in the movement in Russia called "going into the people." The well-to-do, the educated intellectuals, would go into the poor villages to nurse, teach, and do menial chores, in an attempt to bridge the enormous gap between the rich and the millions of peasants. Catherine went on some of these excursions.

Mother was a splendid practical nurse. Twice a week she went into the villages to nurse the sick and the poor. I was her assistant. I would like to have a penny for every mile I walked, carrying a heavy knapsack containing medicines and first-aid needs; for the floors, windows, and doors I scrubbed; for the beds made in sickrooms. Early in my childhood, the truth that Christ is in my neighbor was shown to me by my parents' example and words. (*My Russian Yesterdays*, 12)

The Holy Spirit used these experiences as a child to plant the seed of one of her most fundamental graces: *to personally be where the poor are*, and to help them in whatever way she could. Her favorite gospel text was Matt. 25:31 ff: "I was sick, I was in prison, I was naked." Her inspiration to live with the black people in Harlem flowed from these experiences with her mother.

She learned equally as much about living the gospel from her father. She often related how he would go to the door to meet beggars, bring them to the table, and serve them. From her earliest years, therefore, she was taught, by example, that Christ really and truly was *in the poor*. Failure to see Christ in the other she called "heretical," a word in the West we normally use for wrong doctrine, something wrong in the mind. The Russian spirit sees *a lack of charity* as heretical, that is, a denial of the faith *in practice*. They have an extraordinary awareness of Christ in those who suffer. For Catherine, spirituality must be incarnate, or else it is unreal. (If I am correct, there is no word in Russian for "spirituality," and Catherine did not use it.)

Catherine asked her mother once how she could touch God. Her mother said, "Touch me." She took Catherine to touch God in the poor in the villages. Emma loved the poor so much that she was married among them, in a little village Church, an unprecedented practice in the Russia of that day. Her husband loved her enough to consent. (His side of the family didn't come. But he brought a huge pail of vodka along for the celebration.)

Pregnant with child, Catherine immigrated to Canada in 1921 with her first husband, Boris, whom she had married when she was hardly 15 years old. Remembering the confusion and uncertainties of her own arrival, she would often meet the train in Toronto that was bringing in Russian refugees like herself. She helped them find jobs and places of residence. She and her Russian friends organized a kind of "Russia away from home" colony in Toronto. There Russians could use their culinary, artistic and educational skills to make some money and pass on their heritage to the young and curious. Having become a Catholic, she was shunned by some Russians as a traitor to her country. Thus began another aspect of her passion in this strange land.

In the early 1920s she obtained a job with the famous Chautauqua Circuit whose purpose was to bring culture and entertainment to rural areas. Her act consisted in dressing up in Russian costumes and speaking about that far away and mysterious land that was totally unknown to Westerners. She was very popular—especially when she cried! She discovered that she had a talent for holding the attention of audiences, a gift she never lost.

On the verge of beginning a new lecture bureau of her own in 1929, the Great Depression occurred. It was the last straw. If she could go from nobility to rags, and then from financial security to the Great Depression, was not this life all sand! The Lord was telling her how ephemeral all the foundations of the world were. She finally remembered a promise she had made to God when close to starvation, escaping the Revolution: "If you save my life, I will give it to you." She decided to give up all her possessions and follow Christ in as radical a way as possible.

In the 1930s men were on the streets in Toronto, out of work. She saw the Communists helping and indoctrinating them in Marxism. The Communists had read the papal social encyclicals (she knew, because she went to some of their meetings. This association was a partial cause, later on, of the rumor that she was a Communist). The Communists taunted the Christians: "All talk and no action!" She thought it was time for the Catholics to act.

She started her own group to study these papal social encyclicals. With the permission of Archbishop Neil McNeil she opened a store front and fed bodies with food and minds with Catholic doctrine. She called it Friendship House.

Several Friendship Houses were opened in Canada until the lies of her being a Communist, and misunderstandings in the diocese about her apostolate (Archbishop McNeil had died), eventually forced her to end this first phase of her work for the poor.

Fr. Paul of Graymoor (whom we shall meet shortly) contacted a parish priest he knew working in Harlem, Fr. Mulvoy, about the possibility of Catherine working in Harlem. Fr. Mulvoy asked the advice of Fr. John Lafarge, S.J., the great social activist. He thought it was worth a try. Thus, in 1938, she became one of the first of the Catholic laity to get involved in the interracial justice movement in the United States.

She set up youth clubs, clothing centers, food kitchens, lending libraries. Many enthusiastic young people joined her, as they had in Canada. Her "going into the black people," just as she had done with her mother in Russia, was an ingenious gospel approach. (There is some evidence that President Kennedy got his idea for the Peace Corps from Friendship House, Harlem. His sister, Ethel, used to volunteer at Friendship House. It was her husband, Sargeant Shriver, who was put in charge of the Peace Corps. In her diary Catherine refers to her as "the Kennedy girl.") Invitations came in from other cities. Friendship House soon was in the forefront of interracial justice.

Catherine challenged not only the civil society but the Catholic Church as well, that, in many areas of the country, had not racially integrated their worshipping congregations, educational institutions, or religious orders. She was involved in some of the first sit-ins in America.

On several occasions, in the South, she experienced open hostility. Once she was mobbed on the stage and had to be physically rescued by Blacks. On another occasion, while proclaiming quite forcefully (as was her style) that racial injustice was contrary to the gospel, a bishop got up and said: "Keep Quiet! You can't say those things here." She quietly gathered her notes and walked off the stage—in obedience—but it did not stop her apostolate throughout the rest of the nation.

However, for a second time, in God's providence, this phase of her apostolate was not to last either. The problems this time were internal to the community. Her vision was always very broad, "To Restore All Things to Christ." Many in the community wanted to restrict that vision to interracial justice alone.

Also, her marriage to Eddie Doherty, a nationally famous newspaper man (her first marriage having been annulled), caused some disbelief and hurts. Many were under the impression that Friendship House was a call to the single, celibate vocation. (In hindsight, her decision to marry can now be seen as part of her vocation to remain lay and not become a religious.) The break-up was also due, in part, to her not informing her friends about her intention to marry. Not even her spiritual director knew.

But it was all in God's plan. She went to Combermere, Ontario, with her new husband. They began a newspaper. Catherine continued her outreach to the needy in the area through a clothing room, home nursing, a mail order lending library, and cooperatives. Again, young people were attracted to her powerful faith and love for Christ. Many came to see, and some never left.

A new community grew up around her, and the apostolate expanded. Mission houses were opened in the Yukon to work with the native peoples, in Edmonton and Regina to feed and clothe the needy, in Peru and Bangladesh, to assist the poor in whatever ways were possible.

In the late 60s and beyond, Catherine discerned a new wound in society: loneliness. She opened several what she called "prayer/listening houses" where the community would be available to others for prayer, listening, and counseling.

Always at the heart of her understanding of service was a direct person to person approach. Even if in some of the houses we have rather extensive programs of food and clothing, she always resisted huge, impersonal methods. She experienced, as an immigrant, how impersonal "helping people" could be. She not only wished to help with the necessities of life, but even more with the necessities of the spirit. She wanted to communicate the love of God to others through personal love. This is the spirit she has communicated to Madonna House today.

Presently we have 13 houses throughout North America, and five in other parts of the world—Belgium, Carriacou (West Indies), England, Ghana, and Russia. The apostolates vary from the original soup kitchens mentioned above, to parish work, prayer/listening houses, retreat centers, and a variety of other expressions of both the spiritual and corporal works of mercy. Catherine always wanted the members of the community to be free to engage in any work to which the Spirit might lead them. We have not been founded, therefore, to render a particular kind of service, but to serve, you might say, in a particular kind of way.

What is this way? You may be wondering: "How can you have expertise in everything?" Actually, we don't see ourselves as experts in anything. Everyone brings certain talents and education to the apostolate. The formation consists mostly in how to love in simple ways. Some people may be sent away to complete a nursing course for the needs of the community, or to the seminary to study for the priesthood, or to a language school to prepare for one of the missions. Further professional education is open to us. But presently our apostolates are very simple and unprofessional.

In this sense we're all amateurs, "little lovers," (according to the meaning of the word), not putting the emphasis on our skills but *on our loving*, and using whatever skills we have to manifest the love of God to others. We are constantly amazed at what this love can do. Love is the real healer, the real teacher, the real wisdom. Catherine believed that genuine love of others was at the heart of every attempt to help. On one level our "help" may be, and often is, quite inexpert. And we may have to direct people to get expert help some place else. But often they return to our houses for the love they originally experienced.

One example of many. An AA friend of one of our houses was going through a particularly difficult time. His sponsor said to him, "you have to find a safe place to go through this." He called Madonna House because he said it was the safest place he knew.

"The Restoration of All Things In Christ"

The Russian world Catherine grew up in would still have been permeated by Christian symbols and a Christian atmosphere. Churches were everywhere. Christ was a reality in the homes and mentality of the people. (Not in everyone, of course: that's why there was a revolution. The "intelligentsia" had lost the faith long ago.) But in many ways Russia was still a Christian society: the monasteries were flourishing, the saints were invoked, the icons were carried in magnificent processions, the Czars were crowned by the Patriarch. The Russian word for "peasant" is "Christian."

When she saw Scotland, England, Toronto, and New York in her journey into the West, she must have been vividly (and sorrowfully) struck by what we simply and rather matter-of-factly call "secularization." We who have been raised in a secularized world probably do not think of it as anything unusual. For us it's "normal": in our lifetime, we've never really known any other kind of society. It doesn't shock us as it must have shocked Catherine. "Secular" for her was experienced as "un-Christian."

She was also shocked by the lack of involvement, on the part of Christians, in helping the poor, in confronting the racial injustice of the times. She did not see the presence of the Church in the public square. (On the other hand, by her own admission, she was also acutely aware that the failure of her own country to solve the problem of the injustice to the poor led to the Russian revolution. She was fearful that the same could happen in the West.) She would have been stunned by the compartmentalization of Christianity: people going to Church but generally not involved in having their Christianity penetrate other spheres of their lives.

The books of the renowned sociologist at the Catholic University of America, Fr. Paul Hanley Furfey, especially his *Fire on the Earth*, confirmed her own observation of this compartmentalization of Christianity, as well as giving her inspiration and guidance to do something about it. He eventually became her spiritual director. (cf. below.)

Many of the older members of the Madonna House community have seen the large circular diagram she used to teach this vision: Christ was at the center, and he radiated outwards into every area of human existence. (In my own study of Soloviev I came across just such a diagram which showed how Christ must penetrate the whole of life.)

Combermere

Before she came to Combermere in 1947 she had tried, by the spoken word and by her various works of charity, to achieve this ideal of restoring all things in Christ. But it was always fragmented and partial. When she arrived in Combermere another vision loomed on her spiritual horizon: the total restoration of a Christian culture on a very small scale. In this new beginning she would try, at least in one portion of the vineyard, to create a community life totally immersed in the gospel.

Catherine's way of discerning the Lord's will was to follow him one step at a time. She believed that he spoke in persons and events. When she arrived back in Canada in 1947 with her second husband Eddie Doherty, she didn't have in mind the large establishment one presently sees. But it was in the Lord's mind.

Coming from Russia, she loved the rural aspect of Ontario. She and her first husband had worked with the British forces in Murmansk in 1918. When they arrived in England they were given the choice of emigrating to any country in the Commonwealth. They chose Canada because it was the closest in climate and natural beauty to their beloved Russia. In this context, Catherine often mentioned "the birches."

The Russians love space. In Canada, as in Russia, there was plenty of it: space to plant a garden, trees, and have bee hives; space to have cows and a farm; space to have handicrafts and search for mushrooms. In short, an abundance of space to create something like the estate she grew up on in Russia. In fact, when her brother Andre came to Combermere for the first time, one of his comments was: "Why, this is just like Russia!"

The Christian vision she had carried with her into exile now had the possibility of implementation. Just as her mother taught her how to sew and cook and farm, and that these tasks were holy, so now Catherine taught the young people who came to join her about the dignity of manual labor (a new concept to most North Americans). She taught them home liturgical customs, some from Russia, but some also from their own Western tradition that they had never learned. She taught them that life together was the greatest possible achievement, and that could be exciting, and even fun.

Madonna House, Combermere, is a collection of many buildings, serving the needs of well over a hundred people at any given time. It is without a doubt one of the largest concentrations of people living a dedicated Christian community life in North America. It is a total way of life. It is organized into various departments such as cooking, farming, maintenance, publications, office, and all the other tasks which are necessary for such a large community.

There is liturgy every day, and one of the hours of the Divine Office. (It was the great American liturgist, Dom Virgil Michel, who had visited Friendship House, Toronto, one day, and taught them how to recite the Office. (Praying the Divine Office would have been very unusual for lay people in 1934.) The liturgical seasons and customs permeate the community life.

Our visitors experience 95% of our community life. Catherine believed that the gospel was first of all a way of life, and that it is communicated, first, by living it yourself, and, then, having others share that life with you. (In the Acts of the Apostles, the early Christians described themselves as "the Way.") Practically, this means that the guests work, eat, and recreate with the community. Attitudes and habits in the spirit of the gospel are communicated through personal contact.

Catherine believed that if people could experience the reality of the Christian life, they could then assimilate what they have learned and incarnate it in their own lives and vocations. Then they would be able to communicate it to others. She saw what she called "the community of love" to be, in some real sense, the essence of the apostolate: "If you love one another, then the world will know that you are my disciples." An experience of a community of love is an experience of the way of life Christ came to give us.

Often when people come to Combermere they say it's like "coming home." Whether they know reflectively or not what they are articulating, I'm not sure. Certainly they experience a welcoming community, a home atmosphere, a place of acceptance. On a deeper level they are *experiencing the Church in some life-giving way that they probably have never experienced before.* In some sense, the whole Church is present here—East and West, priests and laity, men and women, parish and diocese—and all infused with harmony and liturgy and a Christian culture.

Here we arrive at the heart of where the Spirit was leading Catherine. Unlike some of the other lay apostolates of the last century, Catherine was being led to form what the Church now calls ecclesial communities. This community is the flowering of her vocation and life. It is not so much her many charitable works that is the crowning achievement of her life, but the ecclesial community she founded, a new model of the Church. All her voluminous teachings are directed to forming members of the Church. It is to the nature of this inspiration of the Spirit we now turn.

What is an Ecclesial Community?

The word the Church is using for some of these movements and communities—"ecclesial"—really says it all. The 20th century has often been called the century of the Church. *Lumen Gentium* is frequently designated as the key document of Vatican II. Throughout the century, and even before, the Popes had been calling for a greater involvement of the laity in the life of the Church. Many people responded to this call. Some of them were truly charismatic persons who attracted followers, and whose apostolates gradually developed into new communities.

A unique dimension, however, of these communities, was that people from other canonical states of life in the Church were also attracted to join them. What the Church and theologians are saying is that people, whether consciously or unconsciously, *were actually seeking a new and life-giving experience of the Church*. This is why many of these new communities do not "fit" canonical forms, because the Spirit is inspiring new models for Church life.

First I will share a quotation from Pope John Paul II's address to the communities and movements gathered in St. Peter's Square in Rome, May 30, 1998. It expresses the Church's present understanding of where the Holy Spirit was leading certain lay apostolates in the 20th century:

> Today a new stage is unfolding before you: that of ecclesial maturity. There is a great need today for mature Christian personalities, conscious of their baptismal identity, of their vocation and mission in the Church and in the world. There is great need for living Christian communities! And here are the movements and the new ecclesial communities: they are the response, given by the Holy Spirit, to this critical challenge at the end of the millennium. You are this providential response! Thanks to this powerful ecclesial experience, wonderful Christian families have come into being which are open to life, true 'domestic churches.' (#2, 222–223)

Next, a rather long quote which expresses this same ecclesial essence of the new communities:

> The experience of the movements only confirms the fundamental precept of *Christifideles Laici* [Pope John Paul's Magna Charta on the mission of the laity], in affirming that to reconstruct the fabric of human society what is needed first of all is to remake the Christian fabric of ecclesial communities themselves.

In this regard I would add that, in contrast to the case of the traditional associations of the lay apostolate, here we are speaking of 'ecclesial movements', both because they welcome the baptized in their various states of life, and because the charisms that arouse and animate them tend to educate in the totality of the Christian, ecclesial experience ('everything in the fragment', according to the expression of Hans Ur von Balthasar, or 'Church in miniature', as one of the movements founders put it.) Not partial, sectarian, fragmentary experiences, not even a particular spirituality, still less the claim of being *the* Church, but rather distinctive reflections of the one Church. Not a fragmentation of the Church, but original, albeit contingent modes of living the mystery of the Church. What a movement embodies and transmits is the life itself of the Church—not just a part of it in some way reduced or 'specialized'. (Guzman Carriquiry, #4, 61)

Not all forms of the lay apostolate have developed into ecclesial communities or movements. However, the Holy Spirit poured out special graces on certain persons in the last century to be the founders and foundresses of these ecclesial communities precisely to manifest different ways of being Church. These persons form a kind of "charismatic coterie" among themselves. Catherine was one of these charismatic persons. Seeing her life in this larger movement of the Spirit is another way of assessing her sanctity and contribution to the Church. While showing you something of the growth of her apostolate into an ecclesial community, I will also share something of her love for the Church. *It was her desire to renew the Church which guided the formation of her community.*

Catherine Answers the Call of the Popes

As was mentioned, in the early 1930s, Catherine began studying, with others, the social encyclicals of the Popes. These writings were calling the laity, in particular, to Christianize all aspects of the modern world. Catherine looked around Catholic parishes and dioceses but didn't see much indication that these calls of the Popes were being implemented. She decided to implement them herself. In her own mind the accent was definitely on *herself*: she didn't envision other people joining her. She understood God's call as that of a lone apostle, "Russian style," trying to implement this call to the laity.

> But it seems to me that I must not hide from myself the truth! A truth which I have known in 1934: that the Apostolate God has called me to has facets I barely can bring myself to look at. Yet I have truly not chosen this Apostolate—it has chosen me! Which simply means God has chosen *me* and no one else to found it. I was convinced that my apostolate, 'my vocation,' was to be a lonely apostolate! He showed me his will by sending me followers! From the very beginning I feared 'foundations,' 'followers,' 'organization.' But inexorably, so it seems, the will of God pointed to this strange—to me—development of what I so firmly thought, felt (was sure of) as my lonely vocation. As a Russian I was attracted to the ethos, the spirituality, of the desert—Nazareth—a desert amidst the people like the Holy Family in the midst of a village. But obviously it was not to be. I had to be a foundress in the Western spirituality's sense of the word! (Diary, April 9, 1965)

Yes, God had other plans. Her zeal and gifts attracted followers, both men and women. In short, a community was forming. In June, 1934, a small group of 16 men and women made simple promises together in St. Michael's Cathedral in Toronto. A few weeks before the ceremony she wrote this prophetic statement in her diary:

> The lay apostolate is the coming event of the Church. More and more it will be at the forefront. Filled with the spirit of Christ it will go and conquer the world. O Lord, give me a small share of that work. Small and simple—but allow me to participate in it, out of love for thee and my neighbor.

1934. This means that Catherine was one of the first in the 20th century whom the Holy Spirit chose to begin a journey towards an ecclesial community, a new expression of the Church.

One of the signs that Catherine was destined to create a new and life-giving expression of the Church is the fact that it was her love for the Church, her desire to make the Church more beautiful as the Bride of Christ, that formed a deep part of her motivation. It's possible to help the poor, work for racial justice, and be involved in all the aspects of the lay apostolate, without the renewal of the Church being too much in the forefront of one's motivation (except in a general way). But Catherine always experienced her vocational call as a longing to make the Church everything She was meant to be.

Already in England (1919–20), before she came to Canada, she was given an understanding of the Church that formed part of her inmost love for Jesus. In a public talk once she said:

> As I grew up I began to understand the Christian idea of the Church. At some point, somewhere along the line, I realized who and what the Church was. I was young, I was in England, and I read something. Suddenly, like a flash, I realized that she was the Spotless Bride of Christ. I saw her clad in the King's robes, beautiful and glorious. This vision stayed in my heart like a warm, consoling thought: the Church was the Bride of Christ, spotless, without blemish, shining, radiant. As scripture says, 'The King's daughter is decked in her chamber with gold-woven robes; in many colored robes she is led to the King.' (Ps. 45:13–14) Yes, my imagination was working overtime. I know that she wasn't clad with just anything. She was something so holy, so precious, something you should die for. This is the Church.
>
> Yes, I understood. I understood the Mystical notion of the nuptials of the Christian with his God. I cannot explain it. It's beyond explanation. But because I entered into the mys-

tery of love which is God, I entered into the mystery of His Church which is his beloved; and I still live in this mystery.

When such things happen to people, then the Church as a mystery, the Church as the Bride, the Church as the People of God, the Church as the Mystical Body of Christ, becomes a reality of faith, for we are in the realm of faith.

From the earliest years, then, Catherine, through her love for the Church, was being led to form one of the ecclesial communities. As her understanding of her vocation grew, so did her realization that she was being called to give some kind of new expression to the life of the Church.

In her diary for May 14, 1965, she was reflecting on the role of priests who were coming to join Madonna House. Her more mature understanding of what the Holy Spirit was doing is exactly what the Church is now saying about ecclesial communities. She wrote:

They [the priests] have been brought to 'a little flock' especially selected, brought into being by God Himself. 'This little flock' is also 'the people of God.' By their coming to MH with the approval of the Bishop, MH now becomes a 'full little church,' or should I say a complete little church,' i.e., Bishop, priests, people of God!

Yet this 'little church' is not a parish, nor a religious order: it is a 'little church on pilgrimage,' on a special pilgrimage, for it has and has not a permanent physical abode. 'It goes where it is needed.'

Historically, such groups often evolved into religious Orders or Congregations. But whenever she found herself veering too close to traditional religious life, the Spirit kept guiding her towards authentic lay spirituality.

What was the inspiration for Catherine's desire to form a community of love, a living expression of the Church? Again, I think her home life was at the root of it. As she said in *My Russian Yesterdays*:

Our joys, our gladness, our fun [at our home in Russia] came from within. They sprang from that sense of security, love, and belonging, which our parents gave us so lavishly. They came, too, from the sense of Order. I spell it deliberately with a capital 'O' because it stems from the great and tranquil *Order of God himself.* When the life of an individual or a family is rooted in that great tranquility of God's order, when its ends are Christocentric, and Faith is an essential part of it, then joy, true laughter, and real gaiety flower abundantly in that individual's or that family's life. Then children grow up in an atmosphere of love and tenderness. Where love is, God is. (13)

This is a simple but accurate description of the vision she had for Combermere. Catherine had experienced a loving family in Russia. After experiencing the revolution and two World wars, and as a result of her long reflection on the Gospel, she knew that *love was the answer to all the world's problems.* She would create a community of love to show that it was possible for the whole world to be such.

I believe that her tragic first marriage was also a powerful impulse to achieve the loving community that she so longed for. In the early years of the Toronto community, and then in Friendship House in the States, she had some experience of forming people into a loving family. She also learned more of what the problems were! Combermere provided the opportunity for developing a community life on a grand scale.

The Trinity

In the last 20 or 30 years, especially in the writings of Popes John Paul II and Benedict XVI—but in many other books and articles as well—there has been a pronounced emphasis on the Blessed Trinity as the ultimate model for the Church, communities, parishes. In my own up-bringing before the Council, I never heard much at all about the Trinity as a model for our life in the Church. I'm sure

I first heard it from Catherine's lips, in the 70s, that the ultimate model for community life was the Blessed Trinity:

> The Eternal Community is the Trinity. It has existed eternally, having no beginning and no end. The Community of the Trinity is simply the Community of Love: God the Father loving God the Son, and this love bringing forth the Holy Spirit. In order to form a community, man must make contact with the Trinity first. Then and only then can he make a community with his fellowmen. (*The Gospel Without Compromise*, 55)

In the very beginning of our Constitution, or Way of Life, she was careful to mention the Trinity:

> At this point I would like to bring to the family that God has deigned to establish through me the very essence of my spirituality, the Trinity, which takes its roots, of course, from Eastern—that is, Russian—spirituality.

Besides seeing the Trinity as our model for unity, Catherine's very dynamic description of the Trinitarian life is very significant for the Christian life. We are not involved here with the Unmoved Mover of Aristotle:

> To me the Trinity is fire, flame and movement. It is like an immense disk from the ends of which shoot out huge flames, the whole of which cover the cosmos. But this is not all. I feel myself being drawn into the center of this fire, flame and movement as if into the eye of a hurricane. (4)

The distinctive spirituality of each of the servants of God flows from his or her understanding of the mysteries of the faith. Catherine's understanding of the trinitarian life was not that of a static, immobile, community of Persons in perfect peace and tranquility. Her God was fire and movement and explosive energy. She reflected this in her life! She said that her whole life had been an attempt to reflect this reality of the Trinity.

Rublev's icon of the Trinity is now frequently seen in Churches, homes, religious establishments. It was not so in the 1950s. Catherine had the trinitarian vision within her from her Russian heritage. And whether it was the frenzy of divine love impelling her to love, or the relations of the Three Persons among themselves, the trinitarian life was the model which she actually sought to express in our lives.

There are two practical dimensions of this theology that our readers may find of particular interest: our authority structure for the community; and the concept of sobornost in electing our directors.

I don't know of any authority structure in the Church, past or present, that is quite like that of Madonna House. We have the three sections of laymen, laywomen and priests, and each of these groups has an elected director. Thus, there is no one authority-head of the whole community. This threesome approach flows from Catherine's trinitarian vision:

> The governing authorities of Madonna House are the Directors General. There is a Director General of women, a Director General of laymen, and a Director General of clergy. The three, like the most Holy Trinity, must be of one mind, one heart and one spirit, each consulting the other on all questions of any importance pertaining to the Apostolate (flock) of which they are the servants. (*Constitution*, 26)

I believe that a number of groups in the Church's history have started out with both men and women members. No doubt one of the big challenges they had to face was men in authority over women, or vice versa. What Catherine was led to—with her face turned towards the Trinity—was a kind of division of authority. In matters which affect the whole community, all three Directors must agree. In matters which affect individuals, the obedience would come from the respective Director. In practice, this means that individuals are under their respective Directors for major, personal aspects of their lives; and the community's direction, as a whole, is guided by all three Directors. So far, it's working!

But in daily life, there will be, and are, many situations where a man may take his obediences from a woman, or vice versa; or a priest from a lay person, or vice versa. A Director of a certain house, for example, may be a man or a woman. Then your obedience, on a day to day basis, is given to that person.

The great key, of course, is to understand that obedience is always given to Christ himself. The frequent changing of superiors is purifying of the virtue of obedience. As we are challenged to obey, now this man, now this woman, now this priest, we are called to go beyond mother- or father-figures, and distorted clerical images. With such shifting and changeable superiors—sometimes daily—one is more and more led to understand that one is always obeying Christ.

As I said above, I have lived in monastic communities, and know something about how obedience functions there. I can testify that our trinitarian arrangement is workable, and is working so far. It is not easy, and has its challenges. But, then, what authority structure doesn't?

I explained this community structure to a monk in an Orthodox monastery once, and he simply said: "It will be more difficult, because it is more of the gospel."

Since we are trying to be Church, one of the graces we have to offer to the Church today is precisely deeper relationships in Christ among men and women, priests and laity, working and living very closely together. "Clericalism" is modified and purified by constant relationships with laity, and by recognizing their gifts. And the new "laicism" (lay people becoming as authoritarian as any priest) is modified and purified by the constant presence of priests, and by respecting their graces of ordination and teaching. The Church is a family. Our authority structure respects the graces of men and women, priests and laity—or at least, is trying to.

The mystery of the Trinity has a "practical" application in how the election of a Director takes place.

Catherine introduced the Russian concept of _sobornost_, unity of mind and heart. The Three Persons are totally one, though distinct as Persons. Whenever some kind of total unity is experienced on earth, a sobornost, an expression of the Trinity, has blessed the earth. (Catherine pointed to Pentecost, the coming of the Holy Spirit upon the infant Church, as an example of sobornost.) "Sobornost originates with the Trinity—Father, Son and Holy Spirit are completely one and they draw us to become one with them and with each other. We are to become as united together as the Father, Son and the Holy Spirit. Sobornost is truly a Trinitarian concept." (_Constitution_, 9)

This unity, in a very real sense, is already a present reality, since the Trinity dwells within each one of us. Sobornost concerns overcoming all the obstacles in relationships so that this unity can be effectively, as well as essentially, present.

In our "Way of Life" she calls us to achieve a total unanimity in the election of a Director. This has not been easy, but so far, with the grace of God, this has been achieved. The theology behind it is that if everyone is truly in a deep relationship of love with God and with one another, the Spirit will inspire all with the same choice.

The goal of our Madonna House spirituality, therefore, in all of our houses, is to form a community of love, with the Trinity as our model. It is not a self-enclosed, turning inward, spirituality, except to meet the God who is within. The apostolic community of Acts 2:42—"faithful to the prayers, the brotherhood, and the breaking of bread"—must be complemented by Matthew 28:19— "Go out into the whole world and preach the good news."

St. Benedict said that the Divine Office, the praise of God, was the Opus Dei, the work of the community. You might say that Catherine *saw love as the opus Dei*, the great work. This love must be accomplished and safeguarded at all costs. If that is not present, the apostolate is dead, and it has lost its reason for being.

These communities, small as they often are, must be places where people experience the love of Christ. They must be open, welcoming. She once described the heart of Madonna House as a warm cup of tea or coffee, and hospitality of the heart. It is not complicated, but it demands a great deal of selflessness on the part of the members.

Catholic Culture

Our houses also attempt to reflect a Catholic/Christian culture. Our Christian homes are the last bastions of freedom. We can, if we will, create atmospheres permeated with the gospel and Christian symbols. The fundamental "divine milieu" Catherine desired for our houses was that of Nazareth.

As the community was growing, Catherine asked the Lord in prayer what really was the essence of Madonna House? She went into the poustinia for five days in May, 1965, and sought some light. When she emerged the answer she gave us was this: "Madonna House is a community of love, like the Holy Family of Nazareth."

She had been amazed at, and had pondered for many years, the mystery of Nazareth. It was her original inspiration to simply live a Nazareth-type life amidst people. And she wondered endlessly: Why did the Lord live so many years of his earthly life in a family in an obscure village?

Well, first of all, that's how most people live—with their families, at home. These are the life cells of the human family. He lived in Nazareth most of his life to emphasize that you can come to the Father right there. To live in love with those with whom you live is the greatest achievement—and probably the hardest. Christ came to give us the power to live in love together. This is the sign that something new is happening in the world. This is the great sacrament. The Holy Family in Nazareth was the perfect reflection of the Trinity on earth. The Trinity and Nazareth—these are the two basic models for our life together.

Our houses outside of North America, however, are not simply North American transplants. We take some of our Combermere traditions with us (which often include customs from other traditions; for example, Our Lady of Guadalupe). But Catherine's charism of striving for "East and West" unity does not simply mean an interiorizing of "Catholic" and "Orthodox" elements, generally understood. This charism, at its heart, is an appreciation for the traditions and cultural expressions of the whole Church, world-wide. Every country to which we are invited has its own saints, its own culture, its own treasures. We try to learn from other Catholic cultures, and reflect them in our houses. This is important.

Catherine said that each of our houses is simply "another room" of Madonna House. But even in our center in Combermere, there is a universality expressed because the Catholic cultures of our houses flow into the center. Our liturgical customs, for example, come from a variety of countries and traditions.

"To Restore All Things In Christ" means making our Catholic heritage come alive once more. We are open to the best of new expressions of Catholicism in the modern world. But so many of our ancient treasures are lying dormant in our books, in our history, in our museums. As the Lord said, "A good householder draws forth from his treasury things both old and new."

Many well-intentioned young people today are cut off from, and therefore ignorant of, any deep spiritual tradition. Peter Berger, the American sociologist of religion, called it, in a book by that title, the heretical imperative.

Because cut off from any living tradition, they are forced to find their own, often heterodox, spirituality. This gives rise to what is now called the "spirituality revolution." I sympathize with them. If I had not been brought up in the Catholic tradition, I don't know where I would be today.

Catherine often said, in the sixties, that the youth were "turning East" because no one had told them about their own profound Western Christian traditions of prayer, silence, and interior disciplines. They flocked to Sai Baba because no one had ever told them about John of the Cross or St.Anthony of the desert. Madonna House seeks to be this place where young people can discover their own spiritual treasures. One outstanding example of our attempt to restore Christian forms of asceticism to these modern God-seekers is the poustinia.

Catherine's book *Poustinia* has sold hundreds of thousands of copies in many languages. It is a call to silence, to prayer, to reflection on the Word of God. On the grounds of Madonna House, in Combermere, we have over 20 small cabins where people may go for a whole day of prayer and silence. (In one field, a row of six stand overlooking a valley. They are to me, sentinels, watching over the world with prayer and fasting and intercession.) These poustinias incarnate, for the young (but not only for them) a means of seeking God that they have not found in any Church of their experience. We have had a number of people who had been involved in the New Age find in Madonna House the treasures they had been seeking. The poustinia is just one example of how we are trying to restore our Catholic culture to the modern world.

Catherine and the Saints

The saints play a very important part in understanding Catherine's spirituality. She called them walking gospels:

in their lives we see how the gospel is concretely lived. She herself learned much from them, and tried to imitate them.

This section will concentrate mostly on the saints of the Western tradition. She had a great love, of course, for the saints of Holy Russia (she had an icon of St. Seraphim of Sarov over her bed). But—if I may put it thus—I find that the Western saints were more like her personal friends. In her writings she speaks of them as intimates, people to whom she prays and to whom she turns in her need. I don't find this same familiarity with the Orthodox saints. In any case, what she says about her saintly Western friends is important for understanding aspects of her own life with God

St. Francis

St. Francis of Assisi was, by far, the most important and beloved saint in her life. Appropriately enough, she met the "tumbler of God" while playing. She was running after a ball in the convent garden in Alexandria. It rolled up to a statue of the Poverello on whose granite arms real birds were perched. "Yes, that is how I fell in love with St. Francis of Assisi—in a convent garden in Egypt. Can any one wonder he has been my friend, my confidante, ever since. He teaches me about love and loving." (*Friendship House*, 47–48) He was her "first love" among the saints. St. Francis led her to one of his other great devotees, Fr. Paul Watson of Graymoor.

In the late 20s she came in contact with Fr. Paul whom I believe was a saint, and for whose canonization I often pray. He was an Episcopalian (Anglican) pastor of a parish. It was through reading the works of Cardinal Newman that he was converted to Catholicism. He had a very great love for St. Francis, naming the Order he founded the Franciscan Friars of the Atonement.

Catherine saw him as a modern day St. Francis. Fr. Paul received Catherine into the Third Order. Through his influence Catherine's devotion to St. Francis grew. She took with her everywhere a small statue of Francis which is still at the front of her desk in her cabin in Combermere.

Fr. Paul had a newspaper called *Ut Unum Sint* for which Catherine often wrote articles about the Third Order. She saw the spirit of Francis as capable of sanctifying the laity in the world. When the first Friendship House was formed in 1934 it was canonically affiliated with Fr. Paul's Order. When public and ecclesiastical opinion turned against her in Toronto, he spoke up strongly on her behalf. Madonna House owes him a great debt of thanks.

The Men in Her Life:
Sts. Ignatius, Augustine, Thomas Aquinas, John Bosco, John of the Cross, Martin de Porres

In the early years of her apostolate in North America there were several other saints who had a strong influence upon her. In her book, *Friendship House*, the last chapter is called, "The Men in My Life," meaning male *saints*. A brief look at each of these men will also be instructive for pointing out some aspects of her spiritual journey.

After meeting St. Francis while playing quite innocently, she recalls how she met another saint in that convent school in Alexandria, this time playing a bit more mischievously.

Catherine wasn't a naughty child. Let us say imaginative, creative—well, a normal, healthy child. She was running through the convent halls—"I shouldn't have been, but I was, and I ran head on into him and knocked him to the floor. He fell with a loud thud and broke into pieces. That gentleman was St. Ignatius of Loyola, of all the people in the world." (Ibid. 148–49) It was the beginning of her association with the Jesuits.

I read once that, for centuries, Russians called all Catholic priests "Jesuits." Catherine the Great had given the Jesuits sanctuary after their Order had been dissolved in the 18th century. (She didn't pay much attention to Papal statements.) They ran educational institutions in Russia. Perhaps they were the only Catholic priests most Russians ever met or knew about. She said St. Ignatius was present on every retreat she ever made.

When she seriously entered upon a spiritual life she often choose Jesuits for directors. One of the first was Fr. Filion, the superior general of the English Jesuits in Canada. Ignatius taught her how to achieve strength of soul, and how serious it is to offend God by sin. Ignatius was her guide through the purgative way: "He shows me the delights of the rugged path. It is he who fashioned the staff of my will, he who shod my feet with the sturdy sandals of clear faith, he who gave me the warm habiliments of penance and mortification." (Ibid. 149)

Significantly, many pages of her early diaries are filled with the Ignatian exercise approach to daily meditation: a reading, reflection, prayers in response, and resolutions. These diaries are an inexhaustible mine of insight into Catherine's spiritual journey. Ignatius was her master in laying the firm foundations of her spiritual life.

A surprising—for me—man in her life, when I first read this Chapter in her book, was the gentleman she met on the eve of fleeing Russia. It was during one of those gray and anxious days when spiritual darkness was descending on Russia. Catherine was listless, restless. She went into her father's library and reached for a familiar book. But it turned out to be another, a new, unfamiliar one, *The Confessions of St. Augustine*. She read for four hours non-stop. "He tore off the veil of his soul for me. He revealed the battles that went on in it against the world, the flesh and the devil. And through it all he sang of the Mercy of God." (Ibid. 151)

Catherine was to have a very tempestuous struggle with God herself. Completely foreign to her was any modern, soft, painless entering into the depths of God. She saw in the lives of the saints like Augustine—and certainly in her own—that the journey to God was painful, a battle-ground. She may also have learned from him that it was acceptable to admit one's struggles, doubts, and fears in the journey to God. (In this sense, Augustine was unique: not many of the Fathers of the Church shared their strug-gles as intimately as he did.)

She was also consoled by Augustine's life: he did not start out as a saint. I will be commenting in Part II about Catherine's Cause for Canonization that is in progress. I think of it here because, as more and more becomes known about Catherine's life, more of her moral failings will come to light. Some will be tempted to say—some are saying it already—"How can she be a saint?"

She loved people like Augustine and Mary Magdalene precisely because they were sinners who finally found a greater Love. She told us countless times that we were saved sinners, and she meant herself first of all. Saints are not people who have never sinned, but living human beings who overcame their sinful tendencies and fell pas-sionately in love with the Beauty they loved all too late.

Another of her directors in Canada was Fr. Henry Carr, Provincial of the Basilian Fathers. He was a Thomist and an educator. He first introduced Catherine, "in cold Canada," to another saint of warm Italy, Thomas Aquinas. Although she never entered upon any serious course of Thomistic studies, she found in Thomas, despite his often abstract profundity, the same fire of divine love she had found in Francis.

What did Thomas teach her? "For the more I got to know him, the more I wanted to know him. He gave me the gift of an intellectual hunger for God, and added one more way in which to love and serve Him better. He walks and talks with me." (Ibid.153–4)

St. Thomas inspired Catherine to become a witness to the gospel by her writings and teachings, as well as by the example of her life. It is noticeable that in the early years of her life, her writings could be quite logical and systematic—like Aquinas. She loved to look up the definitions of words and then give them gospel interpretations; she carefully defined terms and arrived at conclusions. However, in the final and most profound period of her life, this "Thomistic method" changed. In the final thirty years of her life she was taught more directly by the Holy Spirit, and her style is clearly more poetic, unsystematic, flowing from her deeper life with God.

Some of Catherine's statements and teachings, if taken out of context, might be interpreted as being anti-intellectual; or that she was even against the intellectual life itself. Nothing is farther from the truth. Aquinas taught her that exact thinking is also a medium for the truth. She certainly believed that the mind could be dodge and defense against the deeper illumination by the Holy Spirit. She read voraciously.

True, she was insistent that one also had to "put one's head into the heart" to obtain the highest wisdom. One of her favorite quotes was from Aquinas, when he realized, at the end of his life, that everything he had written "was straw." (Mentally I used to note that the Lord had also said to Thomas, from the crucifix, "*Bene scriptsisti de me, Toma,*" "You have written well about me, Thomas.") She didn't often talk about St. Thomas, but he had taught her the excellence of sound thinking, and gave birth within her to this intellectual hunger for God. Francis inspired her with a love for the Crucified; Thomas, with a love for him who said, "I am the Truth."

Another "man in her life" played a key role in her spiritual journey. She came across him in a Catholic pamphlet rack in 1927 when she was making a fair bit of money, but she wasn't happy. "My heart was heavy with unspoken, unfulfilled longings, my soul restless for the mansions of the Lord, my mind in a turmoil of dreams and desires to serve him." The saint she met was John Bosco. His apostolate to youth "crystallized my desires. He, as it were, gave me the compass bearings on the sea of life, pointed to the port I had to reach, and offered to be my guide." (Ibid. 152–3) A few years later she left all and tried to put John Bosco's love for youth and the poor into action. She named her first youth club house for boys in Toronto after him.

St. John of the Cross was the last gentleman she met among these special loves; and the only one introduced to her by a woman, St. Theresa of Avila. It was through her writings that she learned about John. Also, she might have been subject to a general impression at the time—and still now—that St. John is for people in the higher stages of the spiritual life. Her humility, and prudence, would not have prompted her to seek out such an author on her own.

What did she learn from him? "He walks alone and meets one only in the shadows of one's soul. He speaks only through silence. So I am learning to be silent, and silence is hard to put into words. All I know is that I love him, and with all of me I want to listen to him, because he has the words that open secret and hidden paths to the Lord." (Ibid, 154)

He was her guide in the deeper reaches of the spiritual life. As is well known, he is very wary about extraordinary phenomena, and emphasizes the centrality of *faith*. His teaching, combined with the pragmatic and almost anti-mystical tendencies of Ignatius, put Catherine on a very solid basis in her spiritual journey. These are some of the reasons why, later on, in the 1950s, when the Lord began to bestow upon her more profound graces, they strike me, without a doubt, as authentic, because she had gone through the basics of the purgative way, and avoided, with the help of sound spiritual direction, the pitfalls of false mysticism. Several times in her diaries she expresses her legitimate apprehensions regarding mysticism, and her reluctance of being called a mystic.

Because of Catherine's love for the black people in the U.S., she fell in love (a phrase foreign to us but in keeping with her passionate feminine nature) with Martin de Porres as soon as she heard about him. His statue was in the Church across the street from her first apartment in Harlem. She often named her store fronts after him. Her second husband, Eddie Doherty, wrote a life of Martin.

The Women in Her Life: Sts. Catherine of Siena, Theresa of Avila, Mary Magdalen

Significantly, her own patron saint is not Catherine of Alexandria but Catherine of Siena. Someone had given her mother a book about the latter, and she was drawn to her. That she named her daughter after the mystic of Siena is another indication of the two strands of Catholicism and Orthodoxy in the family. (Also, "Catherine" was the name of her husband Theodore's first wife who had died.) Catherine's cabin in Combermere was called "St. Catherine's." A statue of St. Catherine of Siena, upholding the triple crown of the popes, had the most prominent place in her cabin—in the center of the mantel overlooking the fireplace. I don't recall her often mentioning St.Catherine, but that statue said it all: the mystic of Siena upholding the papacy, graced to discern the legitimate Vicar of Christ during a time of great turmoil.

Theresa of Avila appealed to her as the model mystic: one who has her feet on the ground and her head in the heavens. She enjoyed her sense of fun. She loved Mary Magdalen (whose name she took in the Franciscan Third Order), who had sinned much but was forgiven much because of her passionate love. Catherine loved passionate lovers!

Dorothy Day

Dorothy Day is not a canonized saint yet, but we hope one day she will be. (Her Cause is now being considered.) I put her here among the saints because Catherine often said she was one, and would be canonized some day. Dorothy was the contemporary woman who most inspired and influenced Catherine. They were personal friends. Catherine spoke of Dorothy more often than any of the other woman saints mentioned above. One quote (of many possible ones) will give the sense of how powerful this influence was, especially as a companion in suffering opposition:

> But there was another woman who could have cried out just as I did, 'Out of the depths we cry to Thee, O Lord. Hear the voice of our supplications.' That was Dorothy Day. What that woman suffered in the way of rejection is beyond any ability of mine to put into words. Constantly she was rejected by everybody. But she learned the secret of rejection before I did. She was serene and peaceful under blows of that rejection. By the way she accepted rejection she truly taught me as no one has ever taught me. Dorothy Day and Peter Maurin were the shining lights of the 1930s to whom youth came in the thousands to learn the secret of accepting rejections. When she became a pacifist during the war, all her houses dwindled; her rejection was almost complete. She was crucified in the marketplace. I learned much from Dorothy Day. (*Doubts, Loneliness, Rejection*, 78–79)

I can't resist putting in here Catherine's comment that "even during the Second World War, Dorothy stuck to her guns."

Fr. Paul Hanley Furfey

One of the blessings of Combermere, the "little church" that was being born, was the presence of priests.

From about 1951 until her death, Catherine always had spiritual directors. First in the person of Fr. Callahan, then after his death, Fr. Émile Marie Brière, who was perhaps her closest confidante. But before that time she had to search for and find directors. There were years when she was without one. I cannot refrain from saying a bit more about the director who was the most important before she came to Combermere. We owe Fr. Furfey a special debt of gratitude.

He was an outstanding priest of the times, a teacher, and an intellectual, who decried the absence of Catholics in the public square. In those days there really was too much of a "God and me" spirituality, that lacked an apostolic involvement in society. He agreed to be Catherine's spiritual director during a most crucial period of her life— after the break-up of her first Canadian apostolate, and during the foundation and expansion of the Friendship Houses in the United States (1938–43).

We have a very valuable series of correspondence between them, that I hope one day will be published. He doesn't counsel her a great deal about profound dimensions of the spiritual life, but he guided her along a sane, practical path to the formation of her apostolate, and in her relationships and guidance of those joining her. He encouraged her in her strivings to become a saint.

At a certain point, when Catherine was beginning to enter areas of the spiritual life unfamiliar to him, he had the humility to suggest that he had come to the limits of his own discernment and understanding, and that perhaps she should now seek someone else. She doesn't, right away, but I was always impressed by his honesty, humor, practicality, and friendship. He was a providential blessing to our foundress during those crucial years.

"Dear Father"

Again, some of the seeds of Catherine's spirituality were sown in that school in Alexandria. This time, her love for priests. A priest, in his talks there to the children, had mentioned that some people offer their lives for priests. Afterwards, Catherine said she wanted to do this. The priest told her she was too small. The time would come when she wasn't.

I'm sure that in both Orthodoxy and whatever Catholicism she experienced (for example, in Poland, on those visits to her grandmother), a great reverence for priests would have been inculcated in her.

One of her famous and oft-repeated stories—I will tell it in my own words, as we often heard different versions!—is that one day she and her mother came across the village priest drunk on the street. (It might have been in one of those small peasant villages when they went "into the people".) Emma told the horrified little Catherine to help her. They lifted up the hapless father and helped him to his house, put him to bed, and left quietly. There was an awkward silence all the way home, awkward at least for Catherine, not for her mother.

When they got to where they were staying Emma sensed Catherine's possible scandal at what she just witnessed. She told her to go into her bedroom and get the potty from under her bed, wash it, fill it with water, and bring it. When Catherine did so Emma said, "Now go into the garden and bring me a lily." When Catherine brought in the lily Emma put it in the potty and said: "Now, never forget what I'm going to tell you. The potty is the human, sinful, imperfect man. The flower is Christ in the priest. Never confuse the two."

. Later on Catherine would often speak of the Simon and Peter in each priest. "There is a Simon in every priest," she would say, "and we should fear to criticize him lest you touch Peter in him."

Her love for priests was extraordinary because she knew what it was to be without them. She saw one of the last in Petrograd tragically shot.

It was 1918, a dangerous time to have been celebrating Mass. At the moment of the consecration, when the priest lifted up the Host, "the main door flew open. 'Stop that nonsense!' A single shot rang out. Slowly a crimson stain appeared on the back of the white vestment. The priest swayed, then toppled sidewise down the altar step, his out-flung arms letting go of the Host, which rolled slowly, and came to rest on the polished floor of the lower step. The Host was ground into the floor, and 24 hours later the priest was buried." (*Friendship House*, 130–131)

For a year or more afterwards Catherine experienced what it was to be without priests and the sacraments. She was well aware of the sins and weaknesses of priests, but her faith told her that only they could give her the Bread of Life and forgive her sins. "Life for a Catholic without a priest is so tragic, so empty, that it has to be lived to be realized." (Ibid.)

Catherine never in her life wanted to be a priest, but she wanted priests to be priests. If I may be permitted to relate here a powerful lesson Catherine gave to a visiting priest.

A young, zealous padre came to Madonna House once and was seated next to Catherine at table, although he did not know it was Catherine. During the meal he began to speak about going away to study psychology, and how important this was in today's world, and so on. Catherine never looked at him, but as she continued eating she said "Horse shit!"

The priest was most embarrassed, and very angry. He said, "I beg your pardon!" She said, "You heard me, it's all horse shit. If I want advice about law, I go to a lawyer. If I want help with my health, I go to a doctor. If I want to know about God, I go to a priest." Then she said right in his face (as the expression goes), *"Give us God!"*

He told me afterwards that he was angry for two days. After he found out who that "old lady" was, and started to seriously think about what she had said, he concluded that she was right. He never did go to study that all-important psychology. He actually went on to become a kind of Catholic evangelist, speaking to thousands of people about—yes—God.

She didn't think most priests really knew who they were, or what powers they had. If she kissed their hands—which she often did—it was to convey to them what they often forgot: that their hands are anointed, holy, and handle the Bread of Life. If she stood up when they entered a room—which she often did, and which people at a table do when a priest approaches to sit down—it was to remind them and everyone else that Christ's sanctifying power and presence was in them in an extraordinary way.

I recommend, to priests especially (but to everyone, to increase your love for priests) her book, *Dear Father*.

This love for priests has been passed on to the members of the community—the priests members as well! We are human, and everyone struggles with the Simon in the priest, as does the priest himself. But there is a special awareness of the Peter in the priest in Madonna House. How fortunate we are to have 19 priests as full-time members of the community.

Catherine probably never envisioned priests actually joining Madonna House. But the Lord had other plans.

For 30 years she had had priests as spiritual directors, retreat masters, counselors. In the early 1950s, however, through a series of very providential events, Fr. John Callahan, of the diocese of Rochester, N.Y., asked to join. Catherine was overwhelmed. After him, several other priests became members. Another extraordinary phase in this priestly dimension was when one of the laymen, Robert Pelton, asked to become a priest. Catherine was ecstatic. A new phase of Madonna House had begun.

What phase? Becoming Church in a deeper way. A Russian émigré, founding a community on her own in the back woods of Canada, didn't exactly inspire everyone with confidence! Catherine, on her own, might not always have been trusted in her teaching; and often people were not sure of her status in the Church. When Fr. Callahan joined the community, Madonna House achieved a sort of legitimacy in eyes of interested seekers. The presence of the priest allayed the fears of many. Several of our older members told me that they would never have joined Madonna House if priests were not present.

Catherine's love and concern for priests is also expressed in our Associate members—Bishops, priests and deacons. Numbering over 150, Associates find in Madonna House the support of a spiritual family. They receive our cross (which says *pax caritas*), and our community newsletters. Once a year we have a meeting for them in Combermere. Attracted to the spirituality of Madonna House, they seek to live it out in their specific pastoral assignments.

Pope John Paul II specifically encouraged the participation of priests in the new ecclesial "realities":

> Many priests, attracted by the charismatic, pedagogical, community and missionary drive which accompanies the new ecclesial realities, participate in many ecclesial movements alongside the laity. These experiences can be very useful because they are capable of enriching the life of individual priests as well as enlivening the presbyterate with precious gifts.
>
> The positive effectiveness of the movements is revealed when priests find in them the light and warmth which help them mature in a true Christian life, and in particular in a genuine *sensus ecclesiae*, spurring them to greater fidelity to their legitimate Pastors, making them attentive to ecclesiastical discipline and helping them to carry out with missionary zeal the tasks inherent in their ministry. (On the occasion of the Theological Pastoral Convention on "Ecclesial Move-

ments for the New Evangelization," *L'Osservatore Romano*, 11 July, 2001)

The origin of our associate members is worth noting.

Fr. Raya (whom I mentioned above) came to visit. He really didn't want to, but friends dragged him up to Canada. When he saw our cross on Fr. John Callahan, he said he had to have one! He had had a dream about that very same cross. Taking this as a sign from the Lord, Catherine and Fr. Callahan agreed to give Fr. Raya our cross. He is, therefore, the father of all the associates. He fell asleep in the Lord June 10, 2005.

One final expression of Catherine's love for priests is worth mentioning. Around 1980 Catherine had the inspiration to make our community experience in Combermere available to young men seeking to discern a vocation to the priesthood. This was prior to the Vatican's own plea for a propaedeutic year for young men before they enter the seminary.

Every year, then, since 1980, we have had young men come for six months or so, and live in our community. They receive a formation in a simple life-style, prayer, liturgical life, obedience, silence. The priests are available to help in their discernment process. (In reality, they receive discernment from the whole community.) The Holy Father, in the address cited above, notes the usefulness of these ecclesial communities for the formation of seminarians: "The ecclesial movements are also a source of help and support in the journey towards the priesthood, particularly for those who come from specific group situations, with respect for the norms of discipline prescribed by the Church for seminarians."[4]

The Marian Form of Ecclesial Identity

Msgr. Piero Coda, in his important article, "The Ecclesial Movements, Gift of the Spirit," (#4/104) concludes by pointing out that Our Lady's presence is a mark of these movements and communities:

> Von Balthasar has indicated, as a need for the Church today, the rediscovery of the Marian principle: not merely in the sense of renewing devotion to Mary, but in the sense of reawakening in the whole People of God—laity, hierarchy and consecrated—the Marian form of their ecclesial identity. And he recognizes in the movements a stimulus and a providential chance in this direction. 2/104

The fact that Catherine choose, as a name for her community, "Madonna House," the "House of Our Lady," indicates how profoundly she understood what Coda further quotes from Von Balthasar: "Should we not, in our reforms, keep our gaze permanently fixed on Mary, simply to understand what the Church, ecclesial spirit and ecclesial conduct really are?" (Ibid.)

In 1956 Catherine gave the community perhaps her most prophetic talk about the spirit of Madonna House. At the end, one of the priests said: "Catherine, you didn't mention Our Lady!" Never lost for words, she replied:

> Such is the spirit of our Apostolate. Perhaps my silence about Mary was a tribute to the woman wrapped in silence. But I conclude by saying that all that we do in this Apostolate we do through Mary. All of us are consecrated to her as her slaves. That's why we are free. And that is why we can dedicate ourselves so utterly to her Son, because it is she who shows us the Way.

Besides the extraordinary love she brought from her Orthodox tradition, Catherine and her husband Eddie made the Monfort consecration by vow. She testifies in her writings that from that day on, extraordinary growth took place in Madonna House. The Monfort consecration is not required, but it is highly recommended to all the members. She has written books on Mary, including *Our*

Lady's Unknown Mysteries and *Bogodoriza*. She believed that Madonna House was a gift that the Lord had made to his Mother. We belong to her. For us, Our Lady is not simply another devotion. "John Paul II, in a memorable address to the Roman Rota, spoke of the Marian profile as just as—if not more—fundamental and characterizing for the Church as the Petrine one." (#2/103) We seek to integrate our love for Mary at this fundamental level.

Servant of God

I will be describing the Cause for Catherine's canonization more in detail below. Testimonies are coming in from hundreds of people who either knew her or have been influenced by her life and teachings. However, her greatest achievement was the community she founded. All her writings can be understood as profound teachings about forming Christian communities of love, whether as families, parishes, or any other form of the Church's life.

In publicly soliciting testimonies about Catherine over the years, one of the questions I have been asking people is: "If Catherine were canonized, what would be the significance of her life for the Church today?" In official documents, the Church puts the question this way: "What is the pastoral significance of her life?" We have received many responses to this and other questions from Cardinals, Bishops, Priests, Religious and laity. What follows is my brief summary of some of the main replies to this question that highlight the pastoral relevance of her Cause in the minds of those who knew her or about her.

It is well known that John Paul II sought to canonize more lay people. It has been a common criticism for many years that countless religious are canonized out of all proportion to the laity. (In the Commons for the Divine Office we don't even have an Office for a *holy couple*, Sts. Joachim and Anne, for example.)

One reason for this historically may be what scholars of these matters point out: that sainthood became a "social construct" when the Roman process of canonization came into being (11th–12th centuries). This means that holiness had to have certain characteristics. Monks and religious had to be great missionary, learned writers, founders of new Orders. Laity (such as Catherine of Siena) had to have an extraordinary prayer life, perhaps some mystical experiences, or an abundance of charitable works.

But what about deep holiness among the laity down through the ages ala St. Therese of Liseux, that is, a hidden life of extraordinary intimacy with God? Laity did not conform to the accepted model for saints.

The practical problem seems to be that lay people do not have a community behind them to do the necessary work. I think the Congregation for the Saints should somehow address this abnormality. It is inconceivable that there is a lack of heroic holiness among lay people that would warrant their canonization. By the grace of God, Catherine has such a community, but what about all those who do not?

The importance of canonized laity is obvious: most of the Church is lay; heroic sanctity among the laity is a reality; the laity need to see the Church publicly raise lay people to the heights of the altar so they can be encouraged and inspired in their Christian lay vocations. *The lay character of Catherine's life and vocation* would certainly be very significant for the life of the Church if she were canonized.

She was inspired to develop a spirituality that is neither monastic nor religious, but is precisely about loving God in the ordinary tasks of everyday life. Her constant theme, even before it was emphasized by Vatican II, was that holiness is possible in every walk of life. And she especially emphasized—because often not preached or taught very clearly in her day—that lay people could become holy by doing their daily tasks with great love.

Lay Catholics in the post-Vatican II age are more familiar with the Church's teaching which urges them to take up their responsibilities in the marketplaces of the world. In the 1930s it was not generally taught so clearly. Catherine will go down in history as one of the pioneers of the lay apostolate in the Church of the 20th century. It is difficult for us now to imagine how revolutionary and prophetic she was. And she paid the price for it. Her life can serve as a model of lay heroism and dedicated activity as a member of the Church in society.

Married Twice

Catherine's married and family existence went through many stages. It's because she tried to live these stages as a Christian, and maintain her love for God, the Church, and neighbor throughout, that her married life has tremendous relevance for the people of our day.

Her first marriage was very tragic and unhappy. Her husband was unfaithful to her. She was a psychologically battered wife, and knew all the pain of a broken covenant and of trying to raise a child in such circumstances. She didn't handle every situation perfectly. Her son, especially, had wounds from a very confused family situation. She had to go through the travail of obtaining an annulment from the Church, and all the pain that that entails. So many in broken marriages today would find support and consolation in her heroic struggles to remain faithful to God and the Church in such circumstances.

Her second marriage to Eddie Doherty was extremely happy. Thus, she is also able to be a model for the happiness and sanctity of married life: that the love of God must be both the dominant love in marriage, as well as the love that binds the partners in Christ beyond all human ties. This totality of her married experience—the tragic and the joyful—makes her a contemporary witness to fidelity to God in the midst of family circumstances.

After more than a decade of this second marriage, she and her husband decided to give up their conjugal rights and live a celibate life as members of the new community of Madonna House that the Lord was fashioning. Not to imply that this choice is to be imitated, or that it is the "culminating ideal" of married life, but it is one option recognized by the Church. Here too she can serve as a model for those called to this choice in the Lord.

The Social Gospel

A love for the poor and those deprived of their rights has always been a concern of the Church. But especially in our century, the Church herself has called for a "preferential option for the poor." Pope Paul VI has said that there can be "no real peace without justice." Often, if the people of our time do not see this concern for justice in the lives of Christians who are canonized, they do not see any particular relevance of these saints to their own lives in the contemporary situation that cries out for a concern for the poor.

She had the courage not only to help those oppressed by such injustice, but to publicly denounce this practical denial of the Gospel in Church and society. Nor did she simply counsel obedience and patience under the present legal systems. As one imbued with the prophetic spirit, she had a vision beyond time-bound contemporary scenes. She possessed the moral courage of the gospel, teaching that such laws and prejudices were unjust and must be changed. We have in our archives a long report she wrote, at the request of the American bishops, pointing out the racial injustice in Church and society.

She had, all her life, an extraordinary love for the poor. She requested to have on her grave cross the simple phrase, "She loved the poor."

I believe it can be shown from her diaries and personal writings and teachings, that her love for the poor was fired by her love for Christ suffering in them. This has enormous relevance for today when there is so much impersonal and merely humanistic social work. Christ, present and suffering in the other, was at the heart of her spirituality. It was out of this faith and love that her whole life flowed.

I've emphasized (above) her charism to desire, and strive for, the unity of Catholicism and Orthodoxy. She became an harmonious blending, in her own person, of the riches of the East and the West. Her life is a bridge across which many can walk towards greater union and understanding between these two "Sister Churches," (to use the expression of Pope Paul VI). Catherine's canonization, therefore, would have a great relevance for this movement of the Spirit in our time towards the reunion of East and West.

Suffice here to say that, if she were canonized, the people of God would become more aware of the depth and extent of her writings. Even during her lifetime her books were being translated into many languages. What has been published is only a fraction of what one day will be available to the Church. Her canonization would give a great impetus to the influence of her writings. They will immeasurably enrich the life of God's people.

"By their fruits you shall know them." Catherine founded one of the new ecclesial communities in the Church. Her canonization would be a witness to the fact that God continues to inspire new communities in the Church in every age. The spirituality she has bequeathed to this community is, even now, a source of spiritual food and support for thousands of people. In the 60s someone asked her if she had ever received any "words of the Lord" that sort of summed up the essence of her spirituality. She went to her cabin, and pulled out various scraps of paper on which were written what she called her "little mandate" from the Lord. It reads:

Arise—go! Sell all you possess. Give it directly, personally to the poor. Take up my cross (their cross) and follow Me, going to the poor, being poor, being one with them, one with Me.

Little—be always little! Be simple, poor, childlike.

Preach the Gospel with your life—*without compromise!* Listen to the Spirit. He will lead you.

Do little things exceedingly well for love of Me.

Love... love... love, never counting the cost.

Go into the marketplace and stay with Me. Pray, fast. Pray always, fast.

Be hidden. Be a light to your neighbour's feet. Go without fears into the depths of men's hearts. I shall be with you.

Pray always. *I will be your rest.*

Her canonization would increase the spread of this spiritual treasure for the Church universal, and increase the acceptance of the ecclesial communities as a legitimate (and, God willing, permanent) part of the Church's life.

I don't know about you, dear reader, but often, when reading the lives of the saints, I wish they had shared with us more of their struggles and human weaknesses. Do not their doubts, fears and failures inspire us, and give us confidence that we too, who also struggle, can become holy? One of the Fathers said that the doubts of St. Thomas in the Gospel have done more for our faith than all the faith of the other Apostles put together.

When Catherine's diaries are revealed, I think her absolute honesty in revealing her weaknesses and struggles will be one of the greatest blessings for the people of God. Those who have criticisms about her will see that no one was more critical about herself than she. One of the lights shining through her stain glass window will be an incarnation of what the Lord said to St. Paul: "My strength is made perfect in weakness."

C.S. Lewis applied his comment about life being "iconoclastic" to his wife who had died. It will form a fitting conclusion to this brief presentation of Catherine's life:

All reality is iconoclastic. The earthly beloved, even in this life, incessantly triumphs over your mere idea of her. And you want her to; you want her with all her resistances, all her faults, all her unexpectedness. That is, in her foursquare and independent reality. And this, not any image or memory, is what we are to love still, after she's dead. (*A Grief Observed*)

PART TWO

CATHERINE'S CAUSE
FOR CANONIZATION

....

The Catholic Church believes not only that everyone is called to be holy, but that people who have lived lives of heroic sanctity should be publicly recognized. She calls this recognition "canonization." By feasts and devotions, she raises such people before the eyes of the faithful for their admiration, edification and example. This is not to glorify *them* but to acknowledge and praise the power of Christ's grace at work in them.

Many people outside the Church do not understand this practice. However, even a casual acquaintance with other religious traditions reveals that all express a similar human instinct and need by granting recognition to their holy ones. They do not call it "canonization," or designate their holy people "saints" (although some do), but practically it is the same human instinct at work. All traditions have their holy people, their gurus, their sages and spiritual masters, to whom the faithful of those traditions are encouraged to look for edification and guidance.

These holy people would themselves be the very last to want to be praised and held up for veneration. After all, they have spent their whole lives in search of the Holy One, desirous of leading others *to God*, not to themselves.

But we need saints. We need heroes and heroines. What inspires us most in our own spiritual journeys is not clever ideas or theories about holiness, but holy people to whom we can look for example and encouragement. Such people—to speak now of the Catholic tradition—are walking gospels, living embodiments of the sacred tradition. They show us how the gospel can actually be lived out in daily life. Their lives also, then, become another source of gospel wisdom.

St. Gregory of Tours (538–594) was one of the first to compile a compendium of the lives of the saints, the *Liber Vitae Patrum*. He says that he is writing about such people so as "to build up the Church; because the life of the saints not only opens up their intentions but also excites the minds of listeners to emulate them."

The goal of the Christian life is to become holy, to become those living stones which make up the temple wherein God dwells (Ephesians 2:20–22). The purpose of writing about the saints, or raising them up for veneration in the process of canonization, is precisely to build this living temple to God's glory.

Gregory's second point is that knowing the lives of the saints "excites us to emulate them." St. Augustine said that a saint's deeds are a more useful depiction of Christian truth than the employment of complex language in Christian teaching. He should know! As deeds speak louder than words, so the lives of saints speak more clearly and powerfully to us than theories about the moral life. Perhaps some people throughout history were really changed by a *theory* of goodness—those who had the time and leisure to read about it. But who can count the multitude of people whose lives have been changed by the *lives* of the saints, however minimal might have been their knowledge?

This is a theme in some very sophisticated writing today on the moral life. Elizabeth Wyschogrod, in her *Saints and Postmodernism*, writes: "A postmodern ethic must look not to some opposite of ethics, but elsewhere, to life narratives, specifically, those of the saints, defined in terms that defy the normative structure of moral theory." In simpler terms (!) she is saying that contemporary ethical theory has become so helplessly confused and complicated (see also Alistaire Macintyre's *After Virtue*) that the lives of the saints can serve as a living normative pattern for people's search for guidance. (At the end of his book Macintyre says our Western world needs a new St. Benedict. Our new Pope, Benedict XVI, also looks to the Benedictine spirit as one of the sources to restore Europe to its Christian roots.)

For example, any young person can see a movie about St. Francis of Assisi or Gandhi, or read a life of St. Augustine or St. Francis Xavier, and have his or her whole life forever changed by the example of such a powerful personal witness. Even though such a modern young person many not believe in God or Christ—may not even be particularly searching for God—the truth-power of a holy and altruistic life can be life-transforming. The lives of holy people can communicate the Christian message or the height of altruistic human virtue in a direct, forceful and unambiguous way.

Arnold Toynbee, in his great Gifford Lectures published as *An Historian's Approach to Religion*, had this to say:

> A society cannot maintain its social cohesion unless a decisive majority of its members hold in common a number of guiding ideas and ideals. One of the necessary social ideals is a symbolic hero to embody, in a personal form, the recognized goal of the society's endeavors. In the Medieval and Early Modern Western Christendom the West's symbolic ideal figure was the inspired saint (with the chivalrous knight as a secondary alternative). In the Late Modern Age the West has transferred its spiritual allegiance from the inspired saint to the invincible technician, and this change in Western Man's personal ideal has produced changes in his spirit, outlook, and aims. 216

This quote needs no commentary: we need heroes and heroines to embody our ideals. Who will they be?

Another aspect of the purpose of, and the need for, saints, is evangelization. Archbishop Nowak, secretary of the Congregation for the Causes of Saints, said, in an address to people preparing to instruct causes:

> The pope evangelizes with the saints and the blessed, i.e., with the Christians who have lived the faith and the Gospel in an heroic and radical way. They are the evangelical images, true Christians, and to whom we refer for the new evangelization. They are models of the Christian life in the various human conditions which we must incarnate. Their lives are lives of radical testimony to Christ. Today, they are given to us of the new evangelization and to the men and women of our age.

We all know the power of the modern media. It is frequently noted that these media, for better or for worse, will be the main instruments of truth or falsehood in the centuries ahead. If I had a few billion dollars I'd set up a movie company to make great lives of the saints. I would flood the world with images of St. Francis, St. Theresa of Avila, St. Maximilian Kolbe. Great lives, portrayed in powerful, artistically well-done media, would be a tremendous source of inspiration for the world.

I want to take you on a tour of the process of canonization used by the Church, using Catherine as an example. Sometimes fleeting mention is made in the media about a Mother Teresa, or a José de Escriva, Founder of Opus Dei, being canonized. However, few people know much about the process involved. I will, therefore, be presenting Catherine to you as a person being considered by the Church for canonization. Thus I will not present the entire process but only those very early stages of which I, as the postulator for Catherine's cause, have personal experience.

Sometimes I get the criticism that Madonna House is "pushing" Catherine's cause. Catherine is a treasure which has been entrusted to our community of Madonna House in a special way. But she does not belong to us: she belongs to the whole Church. By petitioning to open a cause we are simply seeking the Lord's will concerning Catherine's life and teaching for the "building up of the Church of God."

For the record, the first person to strongly suggest the opening of a cause for Catherine was Archbishop J. N. MacNeil of Edmonton, Alberta, shortly after Catherine's death.

Early Stages in the Process

Canonical work on a person's life, for the purposes of canonization, cannot begin until five year's after that person's death. (Not too long ago—1982—it was 50 years!) The introduction of a cause is a serious affair. It should, therefore, not be initiated immediately after the death of a holy person for fear of emotionalism, misguided zeal, or other confused attitudes which may immediately accompany a death. The modern media, especially, is capable of creating "hype" around important persons. The Church waits to see if the reputation for holiness really flows from the mature faith of the people. There must be time, you might say, for the "dust to settle" so that calm prayer and discernment may have their full sway in such a matter which may be destined to affect the life of the whole Church.

At an appropriate time, therefore, after Catherine's death, the then Directors General of Madonna House, Fr. Robert Pelton, Jean Fox, and Albert Osterberger, asked the Bishop of Pembroke, the Most Rev. Joseph Windle, to approve their appointment of myself as Postulator for Catherine's Cause. In a letter to me dated January 30th, 1991, Bishop Windle wrote: "In accordance with the Norms outlined in the Apostolic Constitution *Divinus Perfectionis Magister* of the Sacred Congregation for the

Causes of Saints, issued on January 25th, 1983, I am pleased to confirm your appointment as Local Postulator in connection with the Introduction of the Cause of the late Mrs. Catherine de Hueck Doherty."

The person or persons initiating a cause is called the *actor*. Actually, any person in the Church has the right to take this initiative. The *actor* is the one who appoints a postulator, approved by the bishop.

What is a postulator (from the Latin word "to ask")? He or she is the person appointed to care for all the legal, procedural and monetary matters relating to a cause. He or she may be a priest, religious, or lay person, competent in theology and the workings of the aforementioned Congregation. (I will be going into each of these steps in more detail later on.) Generally speaking, since my appointment, I have been collecting testimonies of people concerning Catherine's life, gathering materials for the eventual examination by the Bishop's Committee, and endeavoring to learn and follow the proper canonical procedures on the community's behalf. It has been especially important to interview people who may no longer be alive at further stages of the investigation. In fact, some I have interviewed have already died.

Prayer Cards

The Church looks for a "ground swell" arising from God's people as a sign of holiness. It is very common that after a holy person dies the faithful, inspired by the Spirit, begin to ask favors through that person's intercession. Thus the practice has arisen of prayers being composed for this purpose. (It is in the spirit of the process to obtain the Bishop's permission for such prayers.) Some people see such an early move as "pushing a cause." No. While anything like a campaign or media blitz needs to be avoided, discreet ways of making the person known is acceptable, and even encouraged by the Church. A cause cannot proceed, and, more importantly, the Holy Spirit's will cannot be discerned, without some public attempts to make the person known so that an evaluation can be made.

As a community we noted that people were already praying through Catherine's intercession—a sign that the Lord may want to raise her to a more public veneration. So, one of the first things I did was to compose a prayer, asking for favors through Catherine's intercession. Here is the prayer that was approved by Bishop Windle:

> All loving Father, through your beloved Son, Jesus, we have been taught to ask for what we need. And through his spouse, our Mother the Church, we have been instructed to pray for one another and to ask the intercession of your servants who have fallen asleep in Christ. Therefore, through the intercession of your servant, Catherine Doherty, we ask (here mention your petition). We ask this for your honor and glory, and in the name of Jesus Christ, your Son Our Lord. Amen.

Although, in a technical sense, we only pray to God, Catholic piety is filled with many prayers speaking directly to the saints. In the course of my years as postulator, here is another prayer I came across, directed to Catherine herself:

> Dear Catherine of the moment. You, more than most, understood the quietness and smallness of Nazareth. Please come to my aid and comfort.
>
> Somehow, in spite of my love for God, his mother, and you, I have lost my way. My hope is weak. My faith is taunted, and my dreams, dear Catherine, my dreams lie shattered.
>
> Is this his plan for me? Then I accept his will. If it is not, would you plead my cause before the throne of God, and by your holy and practical intercession restore peace to my heart and strength to my faith.
>
> Most particularly, would you intercede for me. *(Here state your special intentions.)* I love you, Catherine. I wish to stay close to you. Please hear my plea and speed relief to me even

as I pray this simple prayer to you, a simple woman. Let me hear God's call as you did.

Some prayers, for example, the one for the Servant of God, Archbishop Fulton Sheen (whom I fervently hope is also canonized some day), only mention a petition for the success of his cause: "Heavenly Father, if it be according to your Divine Will, I ask you to move your Church to glorify your faithful servant, Archbishop Fulton Sheen. I ask this prayer confidently in Jesus' name. Amen." Other prayers, like this excerpt from the prayer for the cause of Elisabeth Bruyere of Ottawa, includes both petitions: "May your servant, model of fidelity to the Church, be glorified according to your will, and may her intercession obtain for us the following favor..... Amen."

All such prayers can only be used privately, that is, not in the public liturgy of the Church (Mass, Benediction, and so on.) "Private" here does not mean "alone" or "not in the Church building." It may be used at other devotional gatherings of the faithful but not in strictly liturgical celebrations. For example, such prayers could be used in a charismatic prayer meeting held in a church. I encourage people to pray this prayer for themselves, with others, or to use it to make a novena. (Some friends of mine have made 54 day novenas using this prayer with quite amazing results.)

I make the point that if they are especially interested in Catherine's cause, to pray only through her intercession. If other holy people are also invoked, the Church cannot use such favors received for Catherine's cause. It will not be clear who the intercessor was. Needless to say, if our Lord or our Lady are also invoked along with Catherine, this is okay since all grace comes through their mediation.

Beware of a Cult

One of the tasks of the postulator is to guard against any premature cult of the person before the proper time. "Cult" has become a negative word in modern parlance, but the Church still uses it in its original meaning. It simply means a display of religious veneration for someone, and this has various degrees. (In the course of my research I came across a fascinating article by the great American convert Orestes Bronson called, "The Worship of the Saints." I was a bit stunned myself at such a use of the word "worship." But he explains how the original English use of the word included a wider range than worship of God. But words do change, and we must be sensitive to that.)

The supreme "cult" is to God. But we also have a cult of Mary and the saints, and each has degrees of meaning and expression. The wrong kind of cult for a Servant of God such as Catherine would include such practices as prayers invoking her in formal liturgical services (as mentioned above); candles before a statue; calling her a "saint," or the day of her death a "feast day"; holy cards with halos, and so on. Also forbidden would be a Mass or Liturgy of the Hours in honor of her; to expose her mortal remains under an altar; or to accord to her relics public devotion reserved only for the saints. The defining characteristic here is "public, ecclesiastical acts." All such practices anticipate the Church's judgment on the person's life and are to be avoided.

One might ask: "What, then, is allowed for a Servant of God?" Well, normal signs of human respect and devotion to someone with a reputation of holiness: flowers or a lamp on the grave; photographs with a prayer asking for the person's canonization, or a request for some grace, as noted above. Relics of the person may be used. (See below.)

A New Bishop

Bishop Windle retired and has since gone to his eternal reward. He gave the cause his enthusiastic support and guided it through its first stages. We will always be very grateful to him.

He was succeeded by the Most Rev. Brendan O'Brien, who saw the process through the next stages, one of which was consulting all the bishops of the region as to whether or not they had any objection to the opening of a cause for Catherine. They did not. (It is a *consultation* not a permission. The bishops of a region may have some reason, socially or even politically, why such a person's cause is not opportune at this time. The competent bishop may still decide to proceed.)

Next, the bishop publishes the postulator's request for the opening of a cause. Bishop O'Brien did this in the Pembroke diocesan paper, asking if anyone had anything, pro or con, to such an opening of a cause for Catherine. The notice read: "Madonna House wishes to introduce the Cause of their Foundress, Mrs. Catherine de Hueck Doherty, to be considered for possible Beatification and Canonization. One of the required steps in this detailed process is for the local Bishop to publicize this request in the diocese and to invite all the faithful to bring to the Bishop's attention any useful information regarding the Cause, which they might have to offer. Accordingly I am inviting anyone who wishes to submit any useful or pertinent information to do so as soon as conveniently possible." No difficulties were encountered.

After these stages, the postulator must draw up a formal request for the opening of the cause. This is called the *Supplex Libellus* (the Written Petition). It contains, in brief, a report on the person's reputation for holiness, life, virtues; a representative collection of favors granted; any obstacles to the cause; a list of all published writings; and a list of witnesses, both favorable and unfavorable. This I did, and formally presented it to Bishop O'Brien.

There are different opinions about just when a cause is opened, and thus when a person can be called "Servant of God." It is the opinion of Msgr. Robert Sarno, one of the canonical experts at the Congregation for the Causes of the Saints (and whom I've met on several occasions), that a cause is opened, and thus one can be called a Servant of God, when the above petition is presented to, and accepted by, the Bishop. After I presented our *Supplex* to Bishop O'Brien, I asked him about the use of this title, and he wrote back: "Catherine can be referred to as 'Servant of God' once the inquiry has been started at the diocesan level. One may refer to her in this way in writings or talks since this is the customary way of referring to those whose cause is under consideration.' Thus Catherine can now be referred to as Servant of God.

On one of my visits in Rome with Msgr. Sarno, he made it clear that my main task, and that of Madonna House, was to gather all the relevant material on Catherine's life for eventual investigation by the Bishop's committee. A very exciting moment was when he wrote out for me (in Latin) the official title on Catherine's file: *Cause of the Beatification and Canonization of the Servant of God Catherine de Hueck Doherty, lay faithful and foundress of the Apostolate called Madonna House.* He continues to be a consultant for me, and to be very generous with his time.

Testimonies

In the *Supplex* (as mentioned) I proposed a list of witnesses to be examined in Catherine's cause. The formal examination of these witnesses is done by the Bishop's committee (which, at the time of this writing, is in the process of being formed). The witnesses are called only after the documents of the person's life have been examined because the questions asked are based on the material uncovered in the person's life.

There is a stipulation, however—"lest any proofs be lost"—that witnesses may be interviewed sooner if there is a possibility that they may not be alive when the formal investigation is in process.

Thus, I have already interviewed a number of people, some of whom have already died (including Catherine's brother Andre). Several general questionnaires are available for this. I added other appropriate questions more specific to the person I was interviewing. A witness must be present for these interviews, and everything is conducted under the seal of confidentiality.

The person being interviewed is not to see the questions beforehand. This helps to insure a more spontaneous, and a less prepared, "researched" response. The relationship of the witnesses to the candidate of the cause conditioned much of the interview. I ask about both the candidate's virtues and faults. The Church is interested in the truth.

After a testimony is transcribed, the person is allowed to read it and make any changes or additions he or she wishes. Then, in the presence of a notary and judge appointed by the bishop, the person signs a statement authenticating that this really was his/her testimony. I probably will be doing more of these testimonies, this "gathering of the fragments," as our community is growing older, and the number of those who knew Catherine is lessening each year.

Kinds of Witnesses

Obviously the most important witnesses are those who personally knew the Servant of God. What I've discovered in interviewing such people is that there is a great variety of views. They all knew the same person, but each had his or her own relationship with Catherine, and each had slightly different insights. Eventually a pattern emerges, a sort of composite picture of the person. Virtues are balanced off with faults, and vice versa. Also, a person's occasional and even fleeting encounter can reveal an aspect of the candidate not noticed in any other encounter. Catherine had a wide variety of relationships. Thus, I believe, a very comprehensive picture of her is emerging.

If people are hesitant to be critical, I purposely ask leading or loaded questions to get their honest opinions. The Church is not surprised that a person had faults. In fact, if the testimonies were too nice, too sanitized, she would be suspicious. Fortunately, in Catherine's case, many people are still alive who knew her. It is emerging very clearly that Catherine was not perfect! (Sometimes community members can emphasize her faults to make sure the people coming after do not have a too perfect idea of her.) One woman, favourable to the cause, wrote: "We don't want perfect saints!"

Next, there are "second-hand witnesses," people who only heard about the Servant of God from others. These people also may not be alive when the Bishop's committee starts functioning, so I collect such testimonies. They have a certain value, although not as important as eye witnesses.

You would think that blood relatives and members of the person's family would have the most accurate knowledge of the person. I have not found this to be true. Or, rather, I should say, that they had intimate knowledge of certain aspects of Catherine's life but not necessarily the most profound, or the most important as far as what the Church is interested in.

In Catherine's case, the people who lived with her in the community she founded have a much more accurate and in-depth knowledge of her than members of her blood family. Often the latter only saw her occasionally, and didn't know the depth of her life with Christ, or much about her apostolic life.

Internet News

The Internet offers a wealth of information, both past and present, on the whole subject of canonization. I don't know how many of my readers have access to this source, but if you do, just type in "canonization" on your favorite search engine and you will have information to your heart's delight. However, I presume many do not have either the time or the facilities for this luxury. I thought I would share with you some scattered pieces of information from the Internet that are relevant to Catherine's Cause. Hopefully you will find them as interesting as I did. As I surf the waves of canonization I swim especially towards items which will help me in my work on Catherine's Cause.

At this writing (2005) Cardinal Martins is the Prefect of the Congregation for the Causes of Saints. He frequently has, on the internet, some reflection on the saints.

The face of Christ shines most intensely in the saints and witnesses of the faith, since in the virtue of their docility to the Spirit, the conformity with Jesus received in baptism appears most clearly in them: they have become more *ipse Christus* [Christ himself] in participating in his life and mission.

But the face of Christ which is reflected in the Saints, and which they have in turn revealed to the world, is that of the Lord who died and rose again, of whom the Pope speaks in *Novo Millennio Ineunte:* 'As on Good Friday and Holy Saturday, the Church pauses in contemplation of this bleeding face, which conceals the life of God and offers salvation to the world. But her contemplation of Christ's face cannot stop at the image of the Crucified one. *He is the risen one.*'

This is what the saints have done. In the variety of their charisms and the plurality of their vocations, they have had the humble boldness to fix their gaze upon the face of the risen Christ, totally living their radical evangelical way of life as a fascinating adventure of the Spirit. They have reached the highest peaks of sanctity, contemplating him with love.

I reflected in Part One on Catherine's charisms. Surely one of the deepest was her generosity in embracing the cross and really finding joy in it. On the other hand, she spoke equally as much about *the resurrection:* "Easter, the greatest feast of the Christian world. It should awaken, arouse, draw, attract, compel, call, every Catholic to arise and become what he truly is—an apostle—one who is sent to preach the glad tidings of the resurrection of the Lord after his incarnation, and what that resurrection means to us."

Thousands of Causes

Most people are not aware that there are approximately 50 or 60 causes of canonization presently in progress in the dioceses of North America alone (and many more hundreds throughout the world). 2,200 cases have already passed what is called the "Diocesan Phase" and are now at the Vatican in the "Roman Phase." A frequent criticism these days is that the Vatican has become a "saints factory." Why this flood of canonizations?

First of all, the "factory" image is not accurate. It implies an assembly line approach: many of exactly the same products rolling off in standardized forms. This is certainly not true. Even a superficial knowledge of the saints reveals the uniqueness of each one. The whole process of canonization is probably the most personalized procedure in the whole world. Intense scrutiny given to all the details of a person's life. One lawyer said that it is the most exacting examination in the world. There is absolutely nothing impersonal, "factory-like" about it.

If the image refers to the quantity of saints being canonized, it is true that more canonizations are taking place than at any other period in the Church's history. There are several reasons for this. The most significant was Pope John Paul II.

> After John Paul II was elected pope in 1978 the pace of canonizations increased so dramatically that in the approximately two decades since John Paul took office almost exactly the same number of people—280—have been made saints as during the previous four centuries. So, if more new saints are wanted, who wants them and why? The answer is easy. It is the Pope who keeps asking for new saints. He feels that the Catholic Church has had many more saints than it to date has recognized and that most of the saints it has recognized reflect a piety too dated, too European and perhaps too passive to provide models of heroic faith that this generation of Catholics need. (Duncan Hanson, *Europe Update*, January 1999)

One of the factors that fueled Pope John Paul's intentions in this matter was his desire to *canonize more lay people* who are contemporary and involved in the needs of society. I noted above the almost heretical mentality present among so many that "real holiness is among the priests and religious." This attitude has partially been fostered by the lack of canonized laity.

Another factor presently speeding up causes of the saints is technology. Within the last 20 or 30 years so much information is now more available on computer discs for those responsible for investigating the lives of candidates. Madonna House is a good example. We are blessed with an excellent archives, and each year more material is being made accessible for the inquiries of the future. It is true: Catherine lived a long time (1896–1985), and she has voluminous writings to be gone through. But the new technology could speed up this examination significantly.

The Pope had also streamlined the process with the Apostolic Constitution *Divinus Perfectionis Magister* (Divine Teacher and Model of Perfection, 1983) which is now the new magna charta for the process. Much more is now done on a diocesan level, bypassing the ancient bottle-neck in Rome. But he believed that there simply *are more holy people in the world that need to be recognized.* He wanted to see canonization much more common in the life of the Church. Heretofore, we have understood it as a rare occurrence. Perhaps sanctity is more common. Pope John Paul thought that it was.

"How Long Will It Take?"

A frequent question people ask me is, "how long is it going to take before Catherine is canonized?" At this point I would say, "Don't hold your breath!" The other day I scanned a list of holy men and women who were born in the 19th century, and whose causes reached the stages of either Blessed or Sainthood in the 20th century. The average time to reach those stages was about 40 or 50 years. There were some exceptions, especially with the martyrs. (I was told at the Congregation for the Saints that the fastest way to become canonized is to burn all your writings and be martyred!) What often makes the headlines are causes which seemed to be "rushed through," such as St. José Escriva and Blessed Mother Teresa; but normally it takes 50 years or more. Usually more.

Canonists distinguish between two types of causes as far as time is concerned: recent and older. A recent cause is when first-hand, eye witnesses with personal knowledge of the candidate, are still alive to testify; an older cause is when first-hand eye-witnesses are no longer living, and testimony is available only from written sources. (If the period between the death of the candidate and the opening of the cause is more than 30 years, the question needs to be asked why so much time was allowed to elapse. Has there been any attempt to hide relevant facts?)

In one case I read about there was a lapse of over 100 years. The living testimony of witnesses who knew the candidate had been broken. Everything must now come from written sources. Such causes may take longer.

Here again, with Catherine's cause, we have another reason to hope for less of a time period. The first steps towards the opening of her cause began after the 5 year waiting period. Very many people who knew her are still alive. The living link of witnesses to Catherine's life is present and unbroken.

A big factor conditioning how long the process of a cause will take is the amount of time and energy the people appointed by the Bishop will have to give to these investigations. The next stage in Catherine's Cause is for the Bishop of Pembroke to set up a committee to investigate Catherine's writings, life, interrogate witnesses, and so on. Competent people, with the proper theological and historical credentials, are often very busy people. They may be able to commit a few years to the work of a cause. Frequently, because of the normal 50 year period of a cause, the task must be passed on to others after a few years. How much time and energy qualified people can give to a cause is a determining factor.

North America, Land of Saints

I mentioned above the number of causes now pending in Canada and the US. This was a pleasant surprise. The following comments would apply equally to Canada and to the US:

'Under past pontiffs, American Catholics haven't thought of saints as something here among us,' says Fr. Gabriel O'Donnell, a Dominican who is postulator—half-chief researcher, half chief lobbyist—for the cause of Fr. Michael McGivney, founder of the Knights of Columbus. 'Part of the problem is that Americans have long had an incorrect idea of the Church's notion of sainthood,' says Fr. Peter Gumpel, a member of the Congregation for the Causes of the Saints, the

Vatican's Saint-making body. 'Rather than limiting its scope to prophets and stigmatics, the Church in the post-Second Vatican Council era is looking for those who have done their duty constantly, joyfully, a person who prayed, who was charitable to others.'

I think it's also fair to say that the *Church herself* is now recognizing heroic virtue among the laity as well as among bishops, priests and religious. (I can't resist this true story. A priest asked a bishop why more parish priests, like John Vianney, are not canonized. The bishop answered: "That's because all the holy priests become bishops.")

A reporter, Delia Gallagher, recently interviewed Cardinal Martins, present head of the Congregations of Causes for the Saints. She asked him why "there never seems to be an American up for canonization."

'A good question,' he laughed. 'The answer is very simple. In countries with an ancient Catholic tradition, sainthood is a part of the very culture, and it is the culture itself which imprints the human, Christian values in which holiness flourishes.'

'So holiness doesn't flourish in the United States,' I ask? 'No, no,' he responds. It certainly flourishes, I have no doubt. But the United States, like England, is a country with a majority Protestant influence. The mentality is different. It is obvious that in those countries, compared to countries that are 99% Catholic, the mentality will be different.'

I think the Cardinal has a point: a culture that still has deep Catholic roots may foster more frequently both the desire for holiness and the means to achieve it. However, we always have to give the Holy Spirit his due. He has raised up extraordinary Christians in mission countries where hardly any Catholic culture existed.

His second reason is probably more of a factor for the deficiency of US canonizations: fewer requests coming from American bishops. "The bishops must take the initiative. I suggest that each of them have one or several competent assistants who can attend to these causes—to examine whether in their churches there are possible cases for beatification and who can assist in the process of bringing these cases to the attention of the Holy See."

There is an American mentality, which may also affect some bishops, that saints and canonization is not the way to go. (Think of the opposition to making Dorothy Day a saint. She even said, "You can't write me off that easily." Or words to that effect.) Some American Catholics think canonization is not very democratic. "Why not have some kind of Hall of Heroes, like the baseball Hall of Fame, which would include others besides Catholics. We don't want to separate our great people from the rest of mankind."

Also, I doubt very much if any diocese in the U.S. has any permanent assistants set aside to look into possible causes. (Has the National Conference of Bishops any such Committee for the Canonization of Saints?)

Generally, Catholics in Canada would be familiar with the famous Saints such as Marguerite D'Youville and Marie of the Incarnation; less so with those "on the way" such as Eleonore Potvin, Theophanius-Leo, or Gerard Raymond. In the United States, most Catholics know of Mother Seton, Frances Xavier Cabrini, Katherine Drexel, Dorothy Day, Bishop Sheen, Fr. Patrick Peyton; less so Mother Mary Theresa Dudzik, Mother Maria Kaupas, Pierre Toussaint, and Angeline McCrory. The youngsters of today will probably see many of the above on the liturgical calendars of the future. My point is that our relatively young Church of North America is also a Church of saints, a Church of holiness, of which we can be very proud.

Relics

Is it not a very human trait to keep mementos of our loved ones—clothing, items which were special to them? Keeping locks of hair of the deceased is not that unusual. And now, with cremation (which I personally don't like), people may even have the ashes of their loved ones in their keeping.

Relics of holy people are a familiar reality to Catholics and Orthodox. But this ancient practice is not mere sentiment or anything simply human. It is bound up with our understanding of the holiness of the body and the communion of saints.

Those who have died are still intimately united with us in the Body of Christ. They are concerned about us and pray for us. Thus, when we touch one of their relics and ask them to pray for us, this is not magic. The relic simply gives us a very human connection with the person, makes him or her more present to us. It helps us to concentrate on their presence and love for us.

A *first class relic* is a part of the person's body—a piece of hair or bone. Through the forward-looking love of some of our community, we have a fair amount of Catherine's hair, although we have been advised, at this stage of the process, not to make these available.

Second class relics are items which have touched the body of the candidate. (We joke that many of us at Madonna House are second-class relics!) Clothing is the most obvious of these. On request, we can send you a second-class relic of Catherine's clothing. It is yours for the asking. I'd rather not ask you for a "donation" for such relics. The distinction between buying a relic or holy service (a Mass), and giving a donation, is very valid, and an ancient practice of the Church. But, as the Reformation proved, it can both be abused by the clergy and misunderstood by others. If you wish, you can always donate to

Catherine's cause in general; there will eventually be many expenses. I'd prefer that we gave out relics for the asking.

Finally there are *third class relics*, items which have touched objects which have touched the body.

Catherine Studies

As Catherine becomes better known, more people are writing about her, researching her life and spirituality. Besides the publications of the community, and numerous articles, a dozen or so more serious, academic studies have been done. Lorene Duquin's, *They Called Her the Baroness* (Alba House), is still the best life of Catherine to date.

Recently (May, 2003), a milestone has been reached in "Catherine Studies." Our associate priest, Fr. Don Guglielmi, of the Bridgeport, Conn, diocese, successfully defended his thesis, and became a Doctor of Sacred Theology. The topic of his thesis? *Staritsa: The Spiritual Maternity of Catherine de Hueck Doherty.* ("Staretz" is the Russian word for "elder" or "wise one.") The significance of this accomplishment is aptly expressed in his own words: "At my doctoral defense Catherine was introduced into the heart of the Church," meaning, Catherine is now known at the highest level of Church scholarship and study. His dissertation director was Fr. Gabriel O'Donnell, O.P., (whom I quoted above). I will present some sections of Fr. Don's thesis. But first, here are some excerpts of his enthusiastic letter to me:

> Well, yes, praise God, it is over and total success. My second reader is a well-known professor of spiritual theology here in Rome, Fr. Paul Murray, O.P. His personal view is important because of his stature in the Roman academic world as a spiritual theologian. He said that when he read the thesis the second time, 'it burns you, like a flame. Her spiri-

tuality shines forth and is a flame.' Isn't that an interesting use of words, just like Catherine!

He also told me that 'for the good of the Church' this must be published. He asked me to consider doing so seriously. He also said, 'I think she is a saint. The holiness of this woman is apparent in this work, and I think she stands a good chance of being beautified.'

So our beloved Catherine has now been introduced to the heart of the Church at one of the oldest pontifical universities in the world—the Angelicum, where the Holy Father received his doctorate. In fact, I defended my thesis today in the very same room where he did so in 1948.

How Fr. Don came to write about Catherine is quite remarkable and worth relating. He had been brought to Combermere in Canada in 1987 by our mutual friends, our associate Deacon Tom Seith and his wife, Monique. Here is his account of how he was led by the Lord to write about Catherine:

In April of 1997 I was at a point in my studies when I needed to choose a topic for my licentiate thesis that could later be expanded into a doctoral dissertation. At first I thought about St. Catherine of Genoa or Walter Hilton, but these would have involved archival work in Genoa or Britain, and seemed too burdensome. After two or three weeks without success, I began to panic as the deadline for choosing a topic approached.

Then one night at the Casa Santa Maria dell'Umilta, where I resided, I had a very vivid dream that changed my life. In the dream I was standing before a larger than life-size outline with four chapters. I 'knew' (i.e., that I was receiving this knowledge from a source outside myself) that the outline was about Catherine Doherty, the Little Mandate, and Madonna House. All this was clear, but I did not know what the outline was, or why I was there looking at it. I walked back and forth, puzzled, and examined it.

Then I noticed that a woman was sitting directly behind the outline. I poked my head around and there was Catherine herself! She was dressed in a lovely blue dress with a flowery pattern that fell below her knees. Her hair was tied back in a bun, and her face was radiant and full of joy and love. I asked her, 'Excuse me, what is this?' She stood up, smiled and pointed her finger towards me, and said, with a thick Russian accent, 'Yes, Father, this is your dissertation. It is going to be easy and quite doable.' I looked at her with amazement, and then woke from my dream.

My heart was burning within me and I wanted to know more about this woman who appeared to me in a dream and gave me my dissertation topic. Noteworthy, Catherine referred to the outline as 'your dissertation,' not a thesis, implying that it would be developed for the doctorate.

After writing down as many details as I could recall, I sent a fax to Fr. Robert Wild, the local postulator of Catherine's Cause, to inquire if writing a thesis about her was in fact, doable. Three days later I received a very positive reply. Then, a friend of mine who was studying for the Legionaries of Christ in Rome called and I told him about the dream. He responded: 'Well, that is very interesting, Father, because for the past two days I have been doing holy hours for you before the Blessed Sacrament, and I asked Jesus to tell you what he wants you to write about because you have been struggling with that.' This was the confirmation I sought. My spiritual director agreed that this sounded like a genuine supernatural dream from God and that I should act on it.'

I will simply pick out certain sections of Fr. Don's thesis which especially exemplify his major theme, Catherine's Spiritual Maternity.

In his Post-Synodal Apostolic Exhortation, *Vita Consecrata*, Pope John Paul II spoke of those called to respond to Christ's invitation to live the Gospel in a more radical way. In the monastic tradition, these men and women were considered 'bearers of the Spirit,' authentically spiritual men and women, capable of endowing history with hidden fruitfulness by unceasing praise and intercession, by spiritual counsels and works of charity.

In addition to living a radical Gospel life in imitation of Christ, their witness was intended to 'transfigure the world and life itself,' through a radical self-renunciation and a ceaseless search for God.' Eastern Orthodox scholar Joseph J. Allen states that 'since the Spirit *does* abide in the Church, it follows that there *will be* an ever-renewing form of bearers or carriers of the Spirit.'

Catherine's formation and spirituality reveal that she may be considered one such contemporary 'bearer of the Spirit.' Her desire to live the Gospel without compromise was a response in faith to the call of God and her contribution to restoring the world to Christ. In addition, as a bearer of the Spirit in the twentieth century, Catherine sought to lead and form others in a radical Gospel life. One way in which she attempted to fulfill this goal was through her spiritual maternity.

This thesis argues that, in the tradition of the desert mothers and the nineteenth century Russian *staritsy,* Catherine exercised a spiritual motherhood to both laity and priests in an effort to lead people closer to God.

In evaluating Catherine's exercise of spiritual maternity we need to make a distinction between spiritual motherhood and spiritual direction in the technical sense. Catherine understood that she was both the founder and a superior of Madonna House. As such, part of her responsibility was to mold and nurture the community in the ways of God and to provide general spiritual instruction on how to live the Gospel without compromise. She did not consider herself a spiritual director, in the classic sense of that term, to anyone at Madonna House, either lay member or priest. Every spiritual director at Madonna House had to be a priest.

Her intention was to respect and preserve the distinction of the role of spiritual director and confessor in the internal forum, and that of spiritual mother, not restricted to the internal forum. Of course, if someone opened his conscience to her, brought her a spiritual problem or question, or asked something in the internal forum, she would answer them with a 'word.'

Catherine understood her spiritual motherhood as one of directing souls aspiring to perfection, but she exercised this ministry in a more general way. Catherine's method of spiritual maternity was quite simple and direct: she provided comprehensive guidance in living the Gospel, addressing herself to the entire community rather than to individual directees. She exercised her spiritual motherhood primarily through her staff letters to the community. In these letters she taught them how to live the Gospel in every aspect of life. She counseled them about Christian attitudes of the heart, Christian behavior, Christian ascetical wisdom and the common good of the community.

If we compare Catherine's qualities as a spiritual mother to those proffered by the tradition, we will see that she possessed all of them: charity, passionate love of God and neighbor, detachment from worldly possessions—and more, a love of poverty, experience of the spiritual life, the dispensing of a 'word' of salvation applied to concrete circumstances and situations, a desire to make Jesus known and loved, humility, discernment, and *to mother Him in others.*

This latter was a significant aspect of Catherine's approach to spiritual maternity, her idea of 'mothering Christ' in others. In one of her spiritual poems, she enters into a dialogue with Jesus about this idea:

Catherine: 'So tell me Beloved. Answer me a question that keeps coming to me again and again. A doctor once told me that I must stop 'mothering,' for I mother You in all I meet and all I can. Is this right, or is it wrong? I cannot stop mothering You in all I meet.'

Jesus: 'You cannot stop mothering me, Catharina mea, for I made you pregnant with myself in many ways. You always are and will be mother, sister and spouse to Me. Priests, men, women, I have begotten through you. In them you mother me and will always, now and in eternity. I have been all things to all men; where the Master is, so should the servant be. But I have ceased to call you servant. You are my friend, hence the friend to all, mother to all, sister to all.'

One of Catherine's most unique contributions was her spiritual motherhood to priests. Catherine called this her 'second vocation'—'my first love is God, and my second love is priests.' God gave Catherine a tremendous capacity to love priests, to spiritually nourish them, and to offer her life as a victim-soul for their salvation. Of particular interest is her poem describing priests as 'little bridges' in great need of repair:

Swiftly I run to my Lord with a heart
full of love and desire.
Desire to make of myself a bridge
For my Lord to cross over.
For behold He said—
'My Father made me a bridge
between himself and man's hunger of Him.
I am *the Bridge*.
But it was my wish to make
many small bridges across the divide
that would carry Me through My Sacrament
to satiate the hunger of man
whom I love so madly
that I made myself helpless
and hidden in bread and in wine
to be carried to all by my bridges.
But behold my little bridges,
My beloved bridges
are falling down.
Go and repair them by making
My sadness your sadness,
My passion your passion,
My pain your pain,
My loneliness, yours.'
I cried out—
'My Love, give me your sadness,
give me your passion,
your loneliness,
and your pain,
and with it give me Your grace
to bear them for I am but nothing
before Thy eyes and have my being only
in the breath of Thy grace.'

She recognized that priests, too, had become spiritual
casualties upon the landscape of a secular culture. Catherine
did not hesitate to undertake this ministry to priestly souls.
Her contribution to them cannot be over-estimated. Her

spiritual motherhood to priests was a factor in saving a number of vocations, and leading others to deeper holiness."

The Many Faces of Stewardship, Letters to the Community, Feb. 3, 1976.

Here is an example of the kind of spiritual maternity Fr. Don is speaking about. Catherine wrote hundreds of letters to her community on every conceivable topic. She speaks here of stewardship:

Time and again Jesus spoke to his followers about the need for stewardship. His parable of the talents in Matthew 25:14–30 is an especially powerful example. If we study the Gospels carefully, we ourselves will come to realize the immensity and all-pervasiveness of that word *stewardship*.

Let us take baptism, for instance. When we are baptized into the life and death of Jesus Christ, we receive a tremendous stewardship. We receive the keys of the Kingdom; and we have the responsibility of opening its doors and of finding out all about it. Because we are the stewards of it, we must seek to penetrate every corner of this Kingdom of ours. We have entered it, not for ourselves alone, but for the whole world. What a tremendous stewardship this is!

This concept of stewardship enters into the nitty-gritty everydayness of my life. I am responsible for so many things. The pollution of the earth begins with me. Do I use sprays that damage the atmosphere? Do I misuse ways of feeding people who are under my care? I am the steward of everything that I use: utensils in the kitchen, books in the library, files in the office, beds in the dormitory.

There is also a stewardship over our bodies. God has created us to be icons of Christ. We can blur the image of Christ in ourselves by being sloppy in our appearance, by having a slouchy posture, by not eating properly, by not disciplining ourselves in all the ways people think they find comfort. If we avoid this self-discipline, then we fail to be stewards over the first and most important gift God has given us—our own incarnation.

We must also be good stewards of our own hearts, and be careful to give Christian example to others. From this springs stewardship of our speech, stewardship of our attention, of our thoughts, of our emotions. This form of self-discipline begins in the heart, but it moves into all the areas of our subconscious and conscious life.

As we learn to guard our hearts properly, we become stewards of our brothers and sisters, of our neighbor who is next to us.

Do you understand what I am getting at? A sense of stewardship is so very important because our lack of it can easily destroy a family relationship, or an entire Apostolate—especially if we fail in *spiritual stewardship*. We must become like those stewards who spend the 'money' of their master wisely. We are entrusted with the money of love, understanding, unselfishness. *Especially unselfishness!* He gives us these gifts out of the great storehouse of his treasures. Let us 'spend' them wisely, not foolishly.

Poustinia: 30 Years Later and On Into the 21st Century

Spiritual fruitfulness is one of the signs the Church looks for in attempting to discern holiness. To repeat what I mentioned at the very beginning: In speaking about Catherine, I never mean to glorify her but the Lord, who is the source of her fruitfulness and whom she always wished to be glorified. "A Christian saint cannot so easily be made into an object of idolatrous worship, because one of the hallmarks of a saint's authenticity is that he should feel and should proclaim that his spiritual achievements are due, not to any spiritual prowess of his own, but to the grace of God working through him." (Toynbee, *An Historian's Approach To Religion*, 227–228) We always invite you to thank God with us for what he has done through her.

Poustinia: 30 Years After

Catherine is probably best known, still today, for her book *Poustinia*. First published in 1975, it was the fruit of her mature life with God. It has inspired hundreds of thousands of people. The depth and power of the words in this book is another sign of God's grace at work in her. (Just the other day I asked a newly arrived guest where she was from. She said the Czech Republic. And how did she hear about Madonna House in the Czech Republic? She said she read *Poustinia*—in Czech!)

Although this year is the 30th anniversary of the book's publication, the inspiration to introduce this Russian tradition of the poustinia into North America occurred sometime in 1961. Thus, even before the publication of the book, there was a long period of the beginnings of the poustinia at Madonna House itself. I would like to share with you not so much the message of *Poustinia* (I hope you will read it if you haven't already) but something of its world-wide and growing influence since its publication.

The community has various opinions about whether Madonna House is a *movement* or not. (The word is usually applied to some of the larger ecclesial families who have thousands of people formally joined to them in some way.) Admittedly we are a relatively small community. However, I believe *Catherine's spirituality is a world-wide movement*, and that, consequently, our Madonna House can be spoken of as a *spiritual movement* in the Church. *Certainly poustinia is that.* I believe that the extent of the book *Poustinia's* influence, briefly indicated here, justifies such an evaluation. (First launched in 2001, Catherine's cause web site averages around 70 visitors per day at the time of this writing, or more than 25,000 visits per year.)

Poustinia is the Russian word for "desert," and it is used to designate a small cabin or room set aside for silence and prayer. After converting an old farm house into a poustinia, a number of small cabins were built in various places on the grounds of the community. Slowly, over the following years, both guests and members of the community would often spend days *in poustinia* in prayer, fasting, and meditating on the scriptures. Several priests and laity began living a poustinik lifestyle: several days "in poustinia" and the other days with the community. At the present time (not counting poustinia rooms) there are about 20 or so poustinia cabins or rooms in Combermere which form an integral part of the community life. I don't know of any other community—ecclesial or otherwise—which gives such prominence to the reality of solitude in its communal structure.

Every one of our houses outside Combermere has poustinia rooms, open to the community members and guests. It is now an integral part of our over-all apostolate. There's so much noise in our society that people can no longer hear the Word of God. We seek to foster a love for silence so people can hear this Word which is different from all other words.

Appreciations of *Poustinia* Outside the Community

A number of years ago the Catholic University of America published a multi-volume work entitled *The Catholic Tradition*. It was an attempt to be an anthology of authors most representative of the Catholic Tradition. The last two volumes are on spirituality. In the last—along with excerpts from the writings of such saints as Francis de Sales, Theresa of Avila and John of the Cross—there is a substantial excerpt from Catherine's *Poustinia*. When I saw this, my own understanding, awareness, and appreciation of God's plan for Catherine in the life of the Church took a quantum leap.

What struck me most of all was the spiritual *stature* of the people with whom Catherine was now being associated. And this high opinion of her life and teaching continues.

For example, there is a very recent book, *The Language of Silence* (Darton, Longman and Todd) by a Camaldolese monk, Peter-Damian Belisle, in Big Sur California. It is part of a fairly prestigious series in England called "Traditions of Christian Spirituality." He treats of many of the great lovers of solitude, beginning with the biblical characters and continuing on to St. Anthony of the Desert, the Carthusians, the Cistercians, Seraphim of Sarov, and many more. And then, in a section of contemporary lovers of silence, he treats of people such as Staretz Silouane of Mt. Athos, Jules Mochanin (the Benedictine in India), and Catherine de Hueck Doherty. He writes:

> Her Madonna House movement [note the word] promoted *poustinia* for the benefit of the Church. Sounding like a desert amma, Catherine wrote that the poustinik fashions the desert into a garden. But the garden was meant to be seen by all. Catherine felt as though she were God's bird sent out to tell the good news to the entire universe. In her wisdom she echoed the ecclesiology of the eleventh-century hermit Peter Damian's *The Lord Be With You* by accenting how the entire Christian community was present to her, and in her. Catherine deeply felt the efficacy of prayer in her poustinia movement—in terms of cosmic dimensions. Her ministry strove to open up contemplation's door to everyone, suggesting *poustinia* to all, and offering *poustinia* for all who might come to Madonna House. Catherine helped to make monastic solitude and silence accessible to everyone, and tried to make contemplation part of everyone's vocabulary. By the end of her life, she considered her entire existence an exercise in poustinia, with her service and ministry being echoes of its solitude and silence. (154–55)

And in a personal note to me, Brother Peter wrote: "What a woman! and a saint."

Before I present a brief survey of the—to me—quite amazing amount of information about poustinia and Catherine available on the internet, let me emphasize that not all of reality is on the internet! In fact, when you consider that hundreds of thousands of people have read the book, surely this means that most of its influence is hidden in human hearts. A few people are able to put something on the internet, but most are not. Just as our real life is "hidden with Christ in God," so most of the graces and fruits flowing from *Poustinia* are hidden in God.

Based on the many personal stories about poustinia that we of the Madonna House community have heard over these many years, and what you will presently read about in my survey of the web, let us together take a brief spiritual journey.

See with your mind's eye the thousands of people who have been and are meditatively reading *Poustinia*, and being drawn to make silence more a part of their lives. Look into homes and see some of the poustinia rooms, or sections of rooms, people have set aside for prayer time. Be amazed at the actual small poustinias people have built on their own property, or on the grounds of religious houses. Walk through retreat centers and see rooms marked "poustinia" for a day of solitude.

I am not making up these examples. I have seen poustinia rooms in basements, over garages, as rooms in homes, in the back of churches. I've seen, and blessed, poustinias built on peoples' property. We ourselves have sold the books and heard the stories. A new depth of silence has settled upon the earth.

All this to emphasize that what I am about to relate from the internet is not the whole story, not even the most important or largest part of the spiritual movement which is *poustinia*. But I must say that I was quite astounded to discover over 200 pages on the Internet dealing with poustinia! (Not to mention the sites which refer to Catherine herself.)

What Is On the Internet?

As would be expected, a good number of sites tell you how to purchase the book. This is highly significant in itself, as the book is still very much in demand 30 years after publication. It has never gone out of print, and we get regular requests.

It is frequently called a "modern classic," and we believe it is. It has been translated into French, Spanish, Italian, Polish, Ukrainian, Czech, Chinese, Korean, Flemish, Portuguese, German, Russian, and Japanese, for a total of more than 130,000 copies.

Quite a few sites advertise poustinia rooms or cabins available for retreats. (Recently it was a thrill for me to see the word "Poustinia" on the door of a room in the Carmelite Centre in Glasgow.) One thing this says to me is that the word and reality of poustinia has become one of the common aspects of the Catholic and Christian prayer scene, a "household word" in prayer circles. Many involved in retreat houses and prayer apostolates would be familiar with poustinia, and now use the word without any longer needing to explain it.

We know of several larger retreat centers where a number of poustinias are available, often for extended periods of time. One, called the Hill of Penuel, is in Belgium, not far from our house near Namur. A small community lives there, with poustinias available for various lengths of time: "Welcome to the Hill of Penuel, a place of silence. You can have access to a prolonged period of prayer, face to face with God. A time of poustinia (desert in Russian), a haven of peace, to discover what is essential."

There are also some personal witness stories about how people received significant graces through their poustinia experience. Several examples.

Fr. Ed Wade, a member of the new Companions of the Cross community in Ottawa, was being interviewed about his decision to join that community.

> Q: Was there any one factor that helped with your decision? Fr. Ed.: I went on a poustinia. The Lord let me know that I needed to make a choice without knowing the far-reaching answers. Getting into poustinia has been a great thing for me: seeing what God is doing in my own heart. I don't have to have all the answers. The Lord is the answer. That quieted me down.

From Joseph de Louw, a Crosier Brother:

> In all the years I lived in Nebraska, I would spend a day in the poustinia. And I must confess I enjoyed it. I was with the Lord, and to do a little fasting and penance. There is something about stepping out of everyday life that reminds you we are on this earth to serve God. Being in the world, people forget that. That's why you spend time as a hermit. Even our Lord spent time alone in the desert.

I found a very valuable review of *Poustinia* by a Russian Orthodox priest of Sts. Cosmos Damian parish in Moscow, Fr. Yakov Krotov. He confirmed for me what I've thought for many years: that Catherine's spirituality (in this case found in *Poustinia*) is not Russian spirituality, pure and simple. In making the point that some of Catherine's ideas are not pure Russian he uses words such as "mistakes," "misunderstandings," "weak points," "all very nice, but...." In other words, he does not find huge errors in her teaching, but not exactly the pure tradition either.

If other Russians agree with Fr. Yakov, it simply confirms my belief that the Lord effected a *new spirituality* in

Catherine's heart. It is not an artificial juxtaposition of Eastern and Western ideas but a new integration of both. Of course, it is not a "new Gospel" but a new expression of the one and only Gospel. One example from his review will show you his general opinion.

> Doherty invents the term 'poustinia in the marketplace' (p.89). She compares the ability to be anchorete [sic] in the marketplace with pregnancy, when a person still continues cooking for her husband, but new life is inside. Applying this example to the mystery of being pregnant with God (and it applies to both men and women), you have, as it were, a 'poustinia within you' (p. 90) All this is very nice, but certainly, the idea of 'poustinia in the marketplace' is not characteristic of the Russian Orthodoxy 'classic' tradition.

I might ask, if I was in a conversation with Fr. Yakov, "What 'classic tradition' do you mean? As you well know, Father, there is quite a variety. Do you mean the classic tradition of St. Nilus Sorska, or of St. Theodosius, or of St. Anthony of the Caves, or of Seraphim of Sarov?" In any case, whether "poustinia in the marketplace" is classic Russian or not, isn't it a beautiful idea! This would be true of much of Catherine's spirituality: it is profound, very rich, a blending of many traditions—and very beautiful.

Generally he says that some of Catherine's ideas about Russian spirituality have been filtered through her western eyes, that is, her western experience. I think this is true. But I'll stop here. I just wanted to emphasize that I've found much valuable material on the Internet about poustinia "30 Years After."

The Glorification of the Saints
in the Orthodox Church

Because Catherine was reared in both the Orthodox and Catholic traditions, and because unity between these two Sister Churches was one of her great desires, Madonna House is interested in the approach to the canonization of saints in the Orthodox Church (and more specifically in the Russian Orthodox Church). Would Catherine's canonization in the Catholic Church be an obstacle of any kind to Russia's openness to Catherine? In her deep heart, Catherine belonged to both the Orthodox and Catholic traditions. (It's my own opinion that she probably didn't think of herself as either Western or Eastern, but as Christian. She wanted to love Jesus, and she incorporated into her spiritual life whatever helped her to do that, as long as it was not in conflict with these two great traditions.)

It is certainly the desire of Madonna House that we also, "in our deep heart," embrace our Orthodox brothers and sisters. We try, therefore, to be sensitive to the great Orthodox tradition. Is "canonizing someone" foreign to this tradition? Would Catherine's canonization be an obstacle to her life and message being accepted by the Russian Orthodox?

A Russian Orthodox understanding of "Saint" may be a good place to begin. The following comes from the pastor of St. Nicholas Russian Church in Dallas, Texas, Fr. Seraphim Holland:

> The word 'Saint' literally means 'Holy One'. We recognize the holiness of those who have struggled to live holy lives, above and beyond the average Christian, by calling them 'Saints.' All Christians are in some sense 'saints', since the word also implies a setting apart. In our Liturgy, the priest exclaims 'Holy Things are for the Holy' shortly before he breaks the Lamb, and this phrase includes all true

(Orthodox) Christians who struggle to be saved, and are indwelt by the Holy Spirit. But when we refer to the 'Saints' we call to mind those who 'fought the good fight and finished the course and kept the faith' (1 Tim. 4:7) and in so doing, have 'labored more abundantly than all of them' (1 Cor 15:10).

God has sometimes revealed to the Church the sanctity of one of His great strugglers. The same Holy Spirit that enlightened the one who 'fought the good fight' also enlightens the Church and uncovers the sanctity of the Saints. At 'a seasonable time' the Church recognizes in an official way that a Christian is a 'Saint', and composes a service honoring them and asking their intercession, and declares a yearly date to observe their memory. The 'glorification' of a newly revealed saint is merely the Church accepting what God has already revealed.

Then he quotes a certain Protopresbyter Michael Pomazansky:

What, in essence, is the Church's formal glorification of saints? Persons who are great in their Christian spirit, glorious in their service to the Church, beacons illuminating the world, leave behind themselves a memory which is not confined to a narrow circle of people, but which is known throughout the whole Church, local or universal.

In witness to the profound certainty of the Church that a reposed righteous man is with the Lord, in the choir of the Saints in the heavenly Church, the Church gives her blessing for the change from prayers for the reposed to prayer *requesting for us his prayerful assistance* before the throne of God. Such is the essence of the act of glorification itself.

Although this term 'canonization' is etymologically derived from the Greek word 'canon,' it forms a part of the terminology of the Latin Church and is not employed by the Orthodox Greeks. This is an indication that we need not use it since the spirit and character of Orthodox glorification is somewhat different from the canonization of the Roman confession. The Roman Church's canonization, in its contemporary form, consists of a solemn proclamation by the Pope: 'We resolve and determine that Blessed N. is a saint, and we enter him in the catalogue of the saints, commanding the whole Church to honor his memory with reverence.' The Orthodox 'numbering among the choir of the saints' has no special, fixed formula, but its essence might be expressed thus: "We confess that N. is in (numbered with) the choir of the saints of God."'

It seems that different Orthodox communions use different words, since I have found, in Orthodox statements, both the words "canonization" and "glorification." If I understand the above quote correctly, our Catholic tradition means the same thing as glorification: When a person is canonized, the Church declares that that person is now in heaven, "numbered among the choir of the saints," and may be invoked in prayer. A liturgy is composed in the person's honor.

In John 17: 5, Jesus prays: "And now, Father, glorify me in your presence with the glory I had with you before the world began." And then, a little later on (v.22) "I have given them the glory that you gave me, that they may be one as we are one." The Eastern Church uses the Lord's own word for what happens when we come into his presence: we receive his glory, are glorified. Our Catholic word canonization refers more to what happens here on earth when someone is declared a saint: he or she is included into the canon of the saints by an act of the Pope. As often is the case, our Roman words are more technical and, yes, canonical, while the Eastern terminology is more poetic, more scriptural.

Recent Examples of Glorification in the Russian Church

Archpriest John Kochurov (1871–1917) was "the first clergyman of the Russian Orthodox Church, whom Our

Lord Jesus Christ made worthy of bearing a martyr's crown in the 20th century from the hands of the godless Bolshevik authorities." (Note the word "canonization" in this official decree): "Proclamation of the Holy Council of Bishops of the Russian Orthodox Church on the Canonization of Archpriest John Kochurov." The Decree then outlines what this means practically. A comparison of these steps with our Catholic practice may be instructive.

1. "That Archpriest John be numbered among the hieromartyrs for Church-wide veneration."

For us also, canonization means insertion in the universal calendar of the Church. The person's veneration is no longer restricted to a particular area or community.

2. "That the righteous remains of the Hieromartyr henceforth be considered holy relics and be left to the care of God's mercy, until such time as they may be uncovered."

At a certain point in our process, a request may be made for the transference of the remains of a Servant of God to another place. There are very specific guidelines for doing this, to assure the identity of the person, and that proper decorum can be observed in the question of relics. Sometimes, in both East and West, the bodies are found to be incorrupt. This is not taken as an absolute sign of a person's "glorification," but it is an added cogent argument.

3. "That the service of the hieromartyr John, following the day of his glorification, be the general service for martyrs and that a blessing is given for the composition of a special service for him."

For us as well, canonization means a Mass and Office may be composed in honor of the new saint.

4. "That the memory of hieromartyr John be celebrated on October 31, according to the Julian Calendar."

The new saint is assigned a date in the universal calendar of the Catholic Church.

5. "That the name of hieromartyr John be included in the synaxis of the new martyrs and confessors of Russia."

6. "That an icon for veneration of the newly glorified hieromartyr John be painted according to the Decree of the Seventh Ecumenical Council."

While pictures of a Servant of God before canonization may be painted, or even medals made, anything—such as a halo—which anticipates the decision of the Church, must be avoided. After canonization, the full religious symbolism of sanctity may be used.

7. "That the life of the hieromartyr John be published for the edification in piety of the Church's faithful."

8. "That, on behalf of the Holy Council, the great and grace-filled joy of the glorification of the new hieromartyr of Russia be announced to the flock of all Rus'."

These steps, for us, would be taken through the offices of the Congregation for the Saints. For example, on May 16, 2004, the canonization of six new saints appeared on the official Vatican website. I was very happy to see, in *The Times* of England, a positive article on one of them, St. Gianna Beretta Molla, the Italian mother who chose between saving her life or that of her child about to be born. She is becoming the icon of the pro-life movement. They also published a large picture of the new Saint holding a baby. There is still some good news in the papers!

9. "That the name of the newly-glorified hieromartyr be made known to the Primates of the sister Orthodox Churches for inclusion in their calendars. Aleksy, Patriarch of Moscow and All Russia and the Members of the Holy Council."

I may be overly ecumenically minded, but I don't see any essential difference between these steps outlined above and the process for canonization in the Catholic Church. I simply conclude that our Catholic canonization of holy people is in keeping also with the present practice of the Russian Orthodox Church.

A few more recent examples of the glorification of saints in the Russian Orthodox Church may also be of interest. On the website *Sobornost: Russian Orthodox Internet-magazine*, I read:

> The bishops' jubilee council going on in Moscow from 13 to 16 August [year?], from Metropolitan Yuvenaly of Krutitsy and Koloma, chairman of the commission on the canonization of saints, regarding results of the commission in the period between meetings of the council. Concerning Metropolitan Yuvenaly's report a decision was made regarding the church-wide veneration in the canon of saints of an assembly of Russian martyrs and confessors of the twentieth century, known by name and hitherto unnamed to the world but known only to God. The council reviewed material about 814 names that are known and 46 heroes whose names could not be determined but it is reliably known that they suffered for the faith of Christ. Evidence for these saints came from 30 dioceses and five stauropigial monasteries.
>
> On 9 October 1989 the Russian Orthodox Holy Bishops Council declared its decision that Patriarch Tikhon of Moscow and all Russia was enrolled in the list of saints of the church. Tikhon had been elected patriarch of the Orthodox Church in Moscow eleven days after the Bolsheviks stormed the Winter Palace in Petrograd in 1917. This man represented steadfast rejection of the socialist revolution. The canonization of Tikhon came in the aftermath of the observance of the millennium of the Christianization of Russia. (Paul Steeves, Berlin Colloquium, May 24, 1996)
>
> The Russian schema-nun Annushka—she who prays with us in heaven—lived a hundred years ago. She was known as a foreseeing and righteous woman. Peoples' memory has passed unto us amazing testimonies of her selfless life in Christ. 'If you love God and the Mother of God, you should also love the sorrows they send you,' she used to say. She was able to feel at a distance the spiritual condition of her children, sending them her prayerful help at the right moment. We collect the testimonies of peoples' veneration, of her miracles and spiritual help for applying to the Synodal

Committee on canonization of saints. (The Novo-Tikhvin, Women's Monastery, Ekaterinburg)

I simply note, therefore, that there is also a process for canonization among the Orthodox. Fr. Michael sums up the Russian's Church's approach to it in this way:

> The glorification of the saints consisted and consists of a general statement of faith by the Church that God Himself has united the departed one to the assembly of His saints. This faith is founded on the facts of a death by martyrdom, or upon a righteous life which is apparent to the whole Church, or upon the glorification of the saint of God by instances of wonderworking during his lifetime or at his tomb. Glorification is usually an expression of the voice of the people of the Church, to whom the higher ecclesiastical authority, after due verification, gives synodally the final word, establishment, recognition, confirmation and the sanction of the Church. (Missionary Leaflet, Holy Protection Russian Orthodox Church)

Around the 11th and 12th centuries, in both the Latin West and the Greek East, a discerning process of canonization began, mostly because of excesses in popular devotion, and because the Church needed more "proofs" of a person's holiness than were being provided locally. Towns would vie with one another in their claims to miracles for their local holy ones. (I believe at one time there were three heads of John the Baptist. This could have been a miracle, but it doesn't seem so!)

An extreme modern example in the Russian Church, for the necessity of such a process, was a crusade, begun in 1990s, to have Rasputin and Ivan the Terrible canonized! In an official statement issued in 2001, Patriarch Alexy II said, not surprisingly: 'This is madness. What believer would want to stay in a Church that equally venerates murderers and martyrs, lechers and saints.' (*The Daily Telegraph*, February 6, 2003).

One other insight from an Orthodox theologian is very fruitful, I think, for fostering union between these two great Churches. It comes from *Creation and Redemption*, Vol. III of the works of George Florovsky:

> Reverently the Church watches for any signs of grace which witness and confirm the earthly struggle of the departed. By an inner sight the Church recognizes both the righteous living and departed, and the feeling of the Church is sealed by the witness of the priesthood of the Church. In this recognition of its brothers and members who have 'attained to perfection' consists the mystical essence of that which in the Christian West is termed the 'canonization of saints,' and which is understood by the Orthodox East as their glorification, magnification and blessedness. And firstly it is a glorification of God, 'wondrous is the Lord in His saints.'
>
> And it is not only to get help and intercession that the Holy Spirit teaches every believer to pray to the glorified saints but also because this calling on them, through communion in prayer, deepens the consciousness of the catholic unity of the Church. In our invocation of the saints our measure of Christian love is exhibited, a living feeling of unanimity and of the power of Church unity is expressed; and, conversely, doubt or inability to feel the intercession of grace and the intervention of saints on our behalf before God witnesses not only to weakening of love and of the brotherly and Church ties and relationships but also to a decrease in the fullness of faith in the Ecumenical value and power of the Incarnation and Resurrection.

I don't have the whole text before me, so I don't know if I am reading my following reflection into Florovsky's beautiful insight. But isn't he saying that the whole Church meets in the saints? Perhaps he is only speaking about the saints of the various Orthodox communions. But would this not apply to the saints of the West as well?

The saints express the unity of the Church in their persons; they have achieved the fullness of Christ. The ancient saying in Orthodox/Catholic relations, that "our divisions do not reach all the way to heaven," has been achieved in the saints. Reverencing the saints of one another's traditions is another way we can share our common life in the Holy Spirit. If we cannot totally agree on doctrine, if we still cannot share the same Eucharist together, can we not reverence together those in both traditions who have joined the choir of the saints?

I had a profound personal experience of this. I was visiting the Russian monastery of Panteleimon on Mt. Athos. It was of special interest for me as it was the monastery of the great modern Russian startez, Silouan. I was with a small group of Greek men who translated for me from English to Greek for the young Russian who was touring us. In the magnificent Church there were many icons of Russian saints such as Boris and Gleb, Seraphim of Sarov, and others. I knew who most of them were, and was walking around reverencing the sacred images.

I think it was because I seemed to know and love these saints that, as I was leaving, our young tour guide motioned me and the others over to a door. He took out his keys and opened it. In the center of the room was a stand with a small wooden box on top. He opened the box. There was a skull in it. I said, "What is this?" He said, "Silouan." I immediately feel to my knees, and so did everyone else. Whatever our differences—we were Russian, Greek Orthodox, and Catholic—at that moment we were all one in the presence of the remains of one who was now glorified in the choir of the saints. This holy man unified us, at least for the time we were together on our knees. The saints can be "sacred spaces" where we experience our unity. They are powerfully praying for this unity in their heavenly choir.

I don't know much about the Orthodox reverence for the saints of the Catholic Church. I know Francis and Benedict and the Little Flower are held in high esteem by many. (I believe the relics of St. Therese were reverenced by some Orthodox as they were taken to different parts of the world.) My guess is that Eastern Saints are more reverenced in Catholicism than vice versa, but I don't really know.

"Are There Any Miracles Yet?"

It is commonly known that approved miracles are part of the Church's process of canonization. For my purposes it is not necessary to go into any complex explanation of what a miracle is. These simple words of Pope John Paul II will suffice:

> Miracles demonstrate the existence of a supernatural order. The universe in which we live is not limited to the range of things accessible to the senses or even to the intellect itself conditioned by sense knowledge. The miracle is a sign that this order is surpassed by the 'power from on high.' The miracles described in the gospel indicate a Power superior to the forces and laws of nature. (General Audience, January 13, 1988)

My emphasis is simply to state that miracles are an essential part of the documentation for canonization. Why is this? In the same talk the Pope answers this question. He mentions the miracles of Christ during his life on earth, especially his resurrection. Such "miracle signs" then continued in the Acts of the Apostles and in the life of the Church down through the ages. He then specifically mentions their occurrence in the lives of the saints and the place of these "signs" in the process of canonization:

> The lives of the saints, the history of the Church and, in particular, the processes for the canonization of the Servants of God, constitute a documentation which, when submitted to the most searching examination of historical criticism and of medical science, confirms the existence of the 'power from on high.' This saving power of the God-Man is manifested

also when the 'miracle signs' are performed through the intercession of individuals, of saints, devout people. (ibid.)

Often when people ask me, "Has a miracle occurred yet?" they seem to be implying (maybe not) that if there is a proven miracle then the canonization will happen next week! At the present time we do not have any report of a miracle which is under serious examination. We are, of course, keeping records of all testimonies relayed to us. But even if such a miracle, through Catherine's intercession, was already proven beyond a shadow of a doubt, this would not really step up the canonization process.

I think that genuine miracles occur often, both inside and outside the Catholic Church. But miracles are not necessarily a proof of a person's holiness. (Recall the Lord's harsh words about some of those who claimed to be performing miracles in his name. He said he did not know who they were. In other words, the power of his name was "working" but their hearts were not with him. Christ made a distinction between his miraculous power working through a person and the person's holiness.

This is why the Church's investigation into a person's holiness of life is really the crucial, the absolutely essential, factor in determining canonization. The Lord can use someone to manifest his miraculous powers even if that person is not leading a heroic Christian life. Only when the Church has pronounced on a person's sanctity does she then seek the Lord's confirmation in a miracle. Life and miracles must go together.

As is well known, two miracles are required. When the Church judges that a person's life has been of heroic sanctity, he or she is given the title of Venerable. A first miracle is then required for the next stage of beatification. This miracle must have occurred after a person's death as canonization technically means a person is in heaven before the Father's face, and the miracle is seen as the Lord's confirmation of the Church's judgment on the person's life.

The second miracle must occur *after one is declared blessed.* The examination is extremely exacting.

> Supporters sort through the reported favors and investigate only the most convincing. The Vatican standard for miracles is extremely high: a board of five doctors, notoriously exacting, must conclude that no reasonable medical explanation exists for a healing. 'Some things that looked pretty miraculous to me were not very good in the eyes of Rome,' says Fr. John Paret, vice postulator for Kateri [Tekawitha's] cause. He has had three proposed miracles rejected; one, regarding a priest who regained vision in one eye after praying to Kateri, was unacceptable because only 90 percent of his sight was restored.
>
> 'We do not accept any cure as a miracle unless we are scientifically, humanely certain that the cure has been instantaneous, not expected, and complete,' says Fr. Peter Gumpel, a member of the Congregation for the Causes of the Saints. 'If God intervenes and works a miracle, he doesn't do it halfway.' 'Some miracles,' he adds ' are better than others. The overnight healing of, say, a third-degree burn is much easier to verify than a complete recovery from cancer. Especially in cancer cases, we require a period of 10 years to see whether the illness will come again, because cancer can go into remission,' he says. (Brendan Koerner 31/01/2003)

Monsignor Michele Di Ruberto is presently (2004) the undersecretary of the Congregation for the Saints. He has spent 35 years in the dicastery, and for the past two decades has been part of the Medical Consultation especially dealing with miracles. He offers some interesting observations:

> To declare someone's holiness is not like conferring an honorary title. Even if someone is in heaven it might be that they are not worthy of public devotion. The process of establishing heroic virtue is not exempt from possible error. We can make mistakes, deceive ourselves. Miracles, instead, can only be realized by God, and God does not deceive.

Consequently, the recognition of a miracle makes it possible to grant with certainty permission for devotion. Hence, the capital importance of keeping miracles as a requirement in the cause of canonization. (Zenit, May 7, 2004)

I found his comment about not everyone who is in heaven may be worthy of public devotion interesting. God, of course, knows everything. In his inscrutable designs he may not wish someone whose life was ostensibly heroic to become an object of universal veneration. There are some saints of the early centuries who were canonized more or less by popular acclaim, without any strict investigation, whose lives we are now discovering might not have passed the present scrutiny for canonization! Probably some of these did not have any miracles attached to their intercession.

After a medical board has given its opinion that a cure was beyond scientific explanation (doctors not being competent to say it was a miracle), the theologians must establish the causative link between the inexplicable cure and the intercession of the person. As mentioned above in praying to the saints, it is important not to pray through the intercession of many or several people. It would not be clear, then, through whom the cure had been obtained. It is within the competence of the theologians to declare such a cure miraculous through a specific intercession.

It may be true that some Blesseds remain so simply because people are not praying through their intercession, and so God is not being "given a chance" to act. I remember that the spiritual director of St. Margaret Mary Alacoque, Bl. Claude de Columbiere, was a Blessed for several centuries because of a lack of a miracle. Then, one day, a priest in California was dying of an incurable disease. A priest friend of his was moved to pray with a relic of Bl. Claude and he was healed instantly. This "pushed him over the top." This is why it is important to encourage people to pray through the intercession of the Servants and Blesseds so that the will of God may be manifest.

You will see in the *Testimonies* section that many graces people attribute to Catherine's intercession are what might be called "moral miracles": conversions of life, a return to the Church, the lifting of a mental illness, to mention only a few. (I think here of Augustine's conversion.) Maybe some day the Congregation for the Saints will figure out a way of accepting *such moral miracles* for causes as well as physical ones. Many of these miracles fulfill the three requirements: instantaneous, beyond human explanation, and lasting.

In the scriptures we have the conversion of Zacchaeus, Mary Magdelen; the apostles giving up everything to follow the Lord. The problem is, how would one actually prove such miracles of the heart? Admittedly they are harder to "prove." But, still, are they not often more astounding? Who can radically change the human heart but God alone?

Testimonies

Helene Iswolsky

Helene Iswolsky was a noted author and personal friend of Catherine's. Both were exiles from Communist Russia. Some of Helene's books include *The Soul of Russia Today* and *Christ in Russia*. Her father was the Russian ambassador to France before the revolution. In her autobiography, *No Time To Grieve*, she wrote of Catherine: "I had the support of a Russian woman who, like myself, was a Catholic, and deeply attached to the Eastern Catholic heritage. She was Catherine de Hueck, known to the American lay apostolate as the 'Baroness,' later Mrs. Eddie Doherty. I had first met Catherine in Paris where she was a reporter for *Sign* magazine, but her main interest was centered in New York. She had just founded 'Friendship House' in Harlem, to promote a true Christian relationship between the white and black people of America. She was a pioneer in a field which in those days, with only a few exceptions, was a subject taboo in American society. She displayed great courage in defending her position" (237).

Maisie Ward

Maisie Ward was the wife of Frank Sheed, and together they founded the Sheed & Ward Catholic Publishing house. She was one of the outstanding lay women of the 20th century. She was deeply interested in, and in touch with, most of the new movements in the Church at that time. She visited Harlem and knew Catherine. Here are some of her comments about Catherine from her autobiography, *Unfinished Business.*

"Catherine's cries of despair and bursts of tears punctuate on page after page [of her books] the stories she tells of human waste and suffering, of spiritual desolation. The witness of Friendship House was its most important act. They battered at the doors of every Catholic college, asking for opportunities for the boys and girls of Harlem. We had rejoiced in both the Catholic Worker [of Dorothy Day] and Friendship House, because they were doing so richly what the world really asks of Catholics in the social field; acting, not just theorizing—and acting with immense self-sacrifice." (pp.246–251, *passim*)

Fr. Richard John Neuhaus

Fr. Neuhaus is Editor-in-Chief of *First Things* magazine, and one of the outstanding thinkers and commentators in the Christian world today. In the December 2000 issue of the magazine, he reflects on his first, and then a more recent visit to, Madonna House.

"[Catherine's] little book, *Dear Father: A Message of Love for Priests*, can be summed up: "Yes, but do you believe, do you really believe, the wonder of who Christ is and you are for him? Show it! Live it!" One is reminded of Chesterton's remark that the only sin is to call a green leaf gray. Catherine railed against a world and a Church that seemed so indifferent to the luminosity of love. (*Dear Father* also contains an excerpt I had quite forgotten from Thomas Merton's *Seven Story Mountain*, in which he tells of Catherine's influence on his vocation.)

"*Poustinia*, perhaps her most influential book, is a strongly moving account of a practice of silence, solitude, and prayer drawn from the Russian experience of pilgrimage and time apart in which a poustinik lives in a small hut—for days or months or years, or for a lifetime—in an isolation that is also total availability to the community. The heart of the poustinia is *kenosis*, joining Christ in the emptying of the self, as described by Paul in Phillipians 2. 'I think that God calls the poustinik to a total purgation, a total self-emptying,' writes Catherine. She cautioned against the impulse to be relevant by doing something useful as the world measures usefulness. 'If you want to see what a "contribution" really is, look at the Man on the cross. That's a contribution. When you are hanging on a cross you can't do anything because you're crucified. That is the essence of a poustinik. That is his or her contribution.' *Poustinia* is one of the more insightful and disturbing books on prayer I have read in a long time.

"As with Dorothy Day, Catherine's 'cause' has been begun. It is possible that somewhere down that path she may formally be declared a saint. Like Dorothy Day, Catherine's faith and piety came to be viewed as 'conservative' because so radically orthodox. (Catherine was baptized in the Russian Orthodox Church and part of the continuing apostolate of Madonna House is reconciliation between East and West, a purpose that is close to the heart of John Paul II.) Both Dorothy and Catherine understood that orthodox Christianity is ever so much more radical than the radicalisms that the world regularly throws up to challenge or recruit Christian faith; and they understood that the way of high adventure is not to trim the Church's teaching but to penetrate ever more deeply into living the mystery of Christ.

"The last half century, and especially the years of this pontificate, has witnessed an astonishing resurgence of renewal movements. Among the better known in North America are Cursillo, Opus Dei, Focolare, Legionaries of Christ, Regnum Christi, and the Neocatechumenal Way. The explosion of similar movements in Latin America and Africa is perhaps without historical precedent. These are mainly movements of lay people, married and celibate, locked in communal determination to live the gospel of Jesus Christ without compromise. The Madonna House Apostolate is part of this remarkable phenomenon. The life of Catherine de Hueck Doherty—in both its pyrotechnical brilliance and silent deeps—begat a movement that has changed lives beyond numbering by its invitation to a disciplined adventure into a revolution of love."

Robert Lax

Robert Lax, a Jew who became a Catholic, was a friend of Thomas Merton's and of Catherine's. In fact, Lax brought Merton to Harlem to meet Catherine. In her book, *Not Without Parables*, in a story entitled, "A Son of Israel," she reflects on her relationship with him: "Yes, I love Jews greatly because Christ was a Jew and so was Mary, his Mother. In Bob Lax I saw both the child of Abraham and the Son of Mary—both Judaism and Christianity. Alleluia!" I once wrote to Lax (who lived on Patmos awaiting the parousia! He has since died), and asked him for a testimony about Catherine.

"Dear Fr. Robert,

"I dream of a long, long letter extolling Catherine's saintly qualities, and it only keeps me from writing the brief note you asked for.

"So, briefly, in answer to your first question: Yes. Her life certainly merits the opening of a Cause.

"Secondly, if she were canonized, what would be the significance of her life for the Church and world of today?

"All the significance a grace-filled, often joyous, dedicated, energetic, tirelessly loving and compassionate, human-divine life can have for the Church and the world and the Heavenly Kingdom now and in eternity. The apparently perfect fusion in her life and personality of well-directed and effective action with constant, profound and deeply loving contemplation and urgent, confident prayer is the quality, the combination of qualities, that I associate first with Catherine.

"May Catherine's Cause prosper, for Heaven's sake, for hers, for ours and for the world's. Robert Lax"

Fr. Godfrey Dieckmann, O.S.B.

Fr. Dieckmann was one of the outstanding liturgists of the 20th century. I knew he had met Catherine on at least one occasion, and through his association with the great Dom Virgil Michel (also of Collegeville), was acquainted with Catherine. In the same book mentioned above (*Not Without Parables*), she also relates her meeting with Dom Michel in the early 1930s: "How does one begin to thank another human being for opening eyes that were still partially sealed? That day Dom Virgil Michel gave us postulants and novices in the then-unknown novitiate of the lay apostolate the *vision of the whole*. He showed us the *whole Christ* who was not crippled by compromise or touched by the fear of human respect.") I wrote and asked Dom Dieckmann for his testimony:

"Dear Fr. Wild,

"I am delighted and grateful to God that the bishop of Pembroke is promoting the Cause of Catherine's beatification (canonization). But whether I can personally contribute anything to the furtherance of the cause seems perhaps unlikely.

"For the simple reason that, though I knew relatively much about her, I personally met her face to face only a few times, and then rather briefly in each case. The first time in the mid-thirties when she came to St. John's to visit the four black young men from Harlem whom Fr. Virgil Michel, O.S.B. had accepted as college students (at a time when few if any Catholic colleges, even in the North, were admitting blacks).

"So I can only report impressions and conclusions from witnessing the powerful influences she exercised on others.

"Impressions: I've met very few people in my life that radiated such vitality and almost overwhelmed you with a contagious *joie de vivre*. She so obviously believed most firmly in her apostolate and knew that the Lord would answer that trust.

"She was the exact opposite of the simpering plastic saints that popular religious art had almost convinced us to regard as 'normal.' She loved life. All of it.

"Conclusion: Perhaps as a consequence of the above character traits she was able to inspire a unique brand of enthusiasts and seemingly unquestioning loyalty and devotion. I think of such persons as Dr. Herbert McKnight (one of the four black students from Harlem of whom I spoke earlier), Betty Schneider (the Chicago Friendship House) and Fr. Peter Nearing. She was a flame that ignited others — for life!

"And that's about it. I'm deeply sorry I can't do more."

Fr. Émile Marie Brière

Our very dear Fr. Émile Marie Brière, Catherine's closest associate, "fell asleep in the Lord," June 16, 2003. I know it would please him to now give his testimony about Catherine and some favors he received through her intercession. Most of us, during her lifetime, just called her "the B" (short for "the Baroness").

"What is it I see in the B? Her faith, trust, humility, love. She is relentless in her pursuit of God. She picks up on everything, that is, corrects everything, so that you will love God more. That is why she gets so impatient with rationalization. She wants you to get to God.

"She is living under inhuman pressures. You think you have problems! You have none in comparison to the B which she faces irrespective of the cross. She doesn't care if people like her or hate her. She could twist everyone of you around her finger, and you would adore her, but you wouldn't adore God. She has a terrific personality, but she loves you too much to draw you to herself, because then you wouldn't love God. You would love her. You would be emotionally, sentimentally, attached to her when she wants you to be strong in love. That would be easy for her to do. She doesn't attract you to herself.

"She is the most tender person I have ever met, understanding of human frailty and human weakness. To her love is complete and full. We are not accustomed to seeing this. The love of B is a very good image of the love of God which is very gentle, very tender and very firm and strong. It isn't the love of a person who doesn't purify. We have to be purified. We have to die to self. We might lead a mediocre life, but in her eyes we are wasting time because we are not loving passionately.

"She is doing all of this constantly under terrific pressures—pressures that are there all the time. That is why she bursts out sometimes. She would like to be more patient. She says publicly that she would like to be more patient. 95% of the time her impatience is due to her eagerness to see someone love God passionately.

"Because there are so many painful experiences in her life, you never know when there will be a strong association with those experiences. She is living under pressure, I would like you to remember. She has many sleepless nights. All this is churning inside her. One of the greatest things is the tremendous sufferings that she underwent during the Revolution. For two or three years she was in very painful circumstances to say the least. A number of her family were killed; that is very painful stuff. She saw the last priest killed; she escaped with her husband.

"But she has never veered one inch in her love. I know these things fairly well. Fiat is her middle name. The Scripture on the 'Valiant Woman' can be applied to B. Her love for you is constant whether she is 'nice' or not. She gets impatient. 'Why doesn't so and so get the picture?' When she loves a person she loves them as they are. She has no animosity toward those who hurt her. She prays for them.

"She trusts in God very simply and directly. Her love is not what we equate with love. We think someone who is "nice" to me, who does things for me — loves me. Her love is a gentle, strong, tender, pitiless love which is the love of God — a shadow of the love of God. She has to discipline us, purify us. Sanctity is possible if we give all and hold back nothing.

"These are the things to look for in B — faith, trust, and her joy. With her the cross is joyful. It is a joyful thing. With her Christ is a real Person. Our Lady, the Blessed Trinity, are very real to her. There is no pietistic stuff. No religiosity, sentimentality. It is from the heart. She loves God passionately. She is very childlike. She has a childlike faith."

Favours Received

We moved my wife 200 miles to the hospital. She had three operations—the third lasted six and a half hours. At this time I appointed Catherine as my wife's head nurse, and left her life in the hands of 'the Head Nurse.' Her condition changed rapidly. In about two weeks she was transferred from Special Care to Rehab. She was then released from the hospital and sent home. The doctor said in a month she will walk on her own. Catherine is now her Head Nurse. —*JM, Tennessee, 7/31/2001*

I firmly believe that the intercession of Catherine has helped me through a major crisis in my life. My business had been in serious trouble for the last few years, and everything was coming to a head this year with the bank beginning to close in on me. Although working and praying very hard for the past 2 years, the solution always remained out of my grasp. As time closed in on me with liquidation and all of its consequences to my wife and children, I began praying every single day to Catherine to intercede for me. I believe that in the final 20 days that I prayed, Catherine's intercession produced the favor that God granted me. The business has been successfully sold, avoiding bankruptcy and allowing me to continue in good, honorable employment for the new owner, with the chance to build it up again. I thank Catherine for her intercession. —*AB, Connecticut*

I have suffered with arthritis for many years. 8 years ago they removed the meniscus from my two knees; also I have suffered from an insufficiency of the veins for at least 30 years. For at least 10 years I have not been able to kneel and get back up again without trying to do so 5 or 6 times. The pain was insupportable, especially at night. I began the novena to Catherine and I improved from day to day.

At the end of a month I left the wheel chair and I have never needed it again. I consider that it is a great healing and it is on the advice of my spiritual director that I write you. Let us give thanks to the Lord, his Mother and Catherine for having interceded with the Father for my cure. I am infinitely grateful for this great grace received gratuitously. —*CB, Quebec*

I wish to share with you some favors that I received through the intercession of Catherine. 1) I was suffering from a severe heart attack three months ago. Now I am very well. 2) There is a lady who was suffering from severe womb trouble; cancer was suspected. I prayed to Catherine on her behalf and when she had surgery she was found to be normal. —*Fr. DJB, Sri Lanka*

I have been praying through Catherine's intercession after my two little boys were murdered and the subsequent suicide of my wife. My grief was devastating and I could find no real relief or understanding of my loss through counseling, medication or associates. I believe Catherine interceded on my behalf, granting me an assured closure in the realization that my little sons are safe and joyful in the hands of God. —*AJ, Toronto, Ontario*

For the past year and a half our granddaughter has been suffering with mental illness and has needed several hospitalizations. About 2 weeks ago, when she was again an in patient, I received the first Cause newsletter and began praying to Catherine for her healing. Last Friday she was discharged and the family is amazed at the change in her. Most common is the remark, "She's herself again." I know that mental healings are hard to verify, but I really believe that this is due to Catherine's prayers. —*AT, New York*

My visit with Catherine was short and to the point. I asked her about starting a house of prayer. She took my hand, closed her eyes, and prayed for a few minutes. When she opened her eyes she said, "Do it!" I was so excited and elated that I ran all the way to the chapel and thanked the Lord whole-heartedly. A great joy. Soon after that I got a call from the Bishop who said, "I have a house for your house of prayer." —*CC, New Jersey, 6/17/2001*

I write today, almost light-heartedly. Two months ago when I was put into prison on remand, denied bail for weeks, and then released and kept in illegal custody, things were grim. Grim! Well, I lost 99.9% of my faith. I came close, so close, to suicide, that it is frightening for a Catholic, a Christian. Then one of the young men who knows me came to the prison. From a collection of papers from an organization he works for he gave me a copy of *Restoration*. 25 years ago I started to read Catherine's books, and enjoyed them on many levels, related to them in many ways. When I read that she is recognized as a Servant of God, I was not surprised. I recognize her as a Saint even now. It might take the Church time to process that, but I believe I do not stand alone in my belief.

I prayed for light, his light. I prayed for justice and freedom. I prayed for the peace I needed to have the courage to battle through what I know will be a court case that could drag on for years considering the red tape and corruption. I used the prayer of intercession as suggested. Did I get a miracle? I was not at death's door physically, but I was close to death mentally and spiritually. I was so close to committing a real sin.

It was almost incredible that in the end I had to spend extra days in prison because of the Court's and the Judge's holidays. I was angry at God over that! It all seemed so unfair after 6 weeks! On Sunday afternoon, knowing that I would be released on Monday, I sat quietly, giving praise to God. Then a total non-Christian came up to me and asked me about my Christian faith. It was just too uncanny. I had found a secluded spot in the prison yard and while reading my Office this man (who had had 6 weeks to ask me about my faith) picked the day before I left! I got such a spiritual lesson out of that that I nearly mentally fainted!

A miracle? I've no idea. I know one thing, though: Catherine's spirit was there with me in that prison. No question about it, no doubt at all. An ageless Catherine, a presence that didn't have age, but had personality, and the person was her, no question. Our small community is aware of this and we are aware that somehow she is with us in our prayers of intercession. —*P, Visakhapatnam, India*

I had clipped out of *Restoration* the prayer to ask for favors through Catherine's intercession. In 1998 I had a diabetic condition. Believe it or not, I no longer take insulin, or pills; and two weeks ago my doctor told me I no longer had to do glucose testing daily. All that I needed to do was see him once a month to check how things were. A miracle? I think so, even though there was work on my part and guidance by the right doctor. It doesn't seem like an accident that this could come about after having to take 52 units of insulin daily. —*BP, Ontario*

My sister-in-law was visiting. She asked if she could use Catherine's relic on my ear, and some prayers were said. I felt my ear pop and was getting relief. After a few days I am feeling better. —*C, Ontario*

A friend had a massive heart attack. I laid a relic of Catherine on his arm and was rewarded with a big smile. But then for three weeks afterwards he was in a coma. The doctors recommended that the family should think about taking him off the ventilator. They asked me what to do and I said I couldn't make a suggestion or decision. I prayed again with Catherine's relic that God would bring him back to full health, or take him before the family had to make a decision. The day after we received a call. Miracle! Miracle! Dad became alert enough to understand what was going on and the doctor was able to ask him if he wanted the tube out and to try just breathing with the help of oxygen. He said he did. The doctor also asked if he wanted it back in if he couldn't breathe, and he said yes to that too. The decision became his and no one else had to fret or feel guilty that they were pulling the plug on their beloved. We are so grateful! God love Catherine! —*MB, Windsor, Ontario*

My husband and my son went three years without talking with each other or seeing each other. Every Monday, in the house of a friend, we prayed the rosary and, as I have a relic of Catherine, we begged her intercession. It was through these prayers that one day my husband decided to open his heart and go to the house of our son. Until then our son had not wanted to receive him. The two conversed and today they are good friends. It is hard to imagine the power of the intercession of a Servant of God! May the Immaculate Heart of Mary and the intercession of Catherine pour blessings over all of you. —*SFQ, Sao Carlos, Brazil*

We were praying for my husband and I to conceive. We just received our Christmas miracle and we know that it was through the intercession of the Servant of God Catherine Doherty. I just wanted to thank you all and let you know that Catherine is truly a servant of God. We know that we are truly blessed with this little bundle of joy who is definitely a Christmas miracle. —*MT*

I believe that I received a favor through Catherine's intercession. For the past three weeks I had been experiencing mild depression. My daughter was currently visiting Madonna House in Combermere and she called me.

She said that she had visited Catherine's grave that day, put her hand on the cross above her grave, and prayed for me. It wasn't until a few hours later on in the afternoon that I realized that I was feeling better, like this depression had lifted. I have to say that I had been praying as well, but I feel sure that Catherine had a lot to do with it. — *(No name)*

I was diagnosed with breast cancer around May, 1998, at the age of 76. Before I had surgery in September I started praying to Catherine, asking for her help. I had the surgery in September and since then I have had good reports. Thanks to Our Lady and Catherine. —*UB, Combermere, Ontario.*

I believe my brother was healed of prostate cancer as a result of Catherine's intercession. I firmly believe the healing was done by Catherine's help. I felt enlightened, my worries disappeared right after asking for this favor. — *MM, Alexandria, Ontario*

Catherine's Falling Asleep in the Lord

It took a long time for the theme of how to end this book came together in my heart. But I think it will be very meaningful for you, dear reader and friend of Catherine. What came to me in prayer in the poustinia was this: I bet not many people have ever read the eye-witness account of Catherine's death, written by the two community members who were actually with her that night.

"Falling asleep in the Lord." It's a beautiful expression, isn't it, from the early church. Not all Christian deaths are free from pain. But even when Stephen was stoned to death—a terrible kind of execution—the Scripture says—

amazingly—"and with these words he fell asleep" (Acts 8:60).

As you will see in their accounts, by the mercy of God, Catherine too simply "fell asleep in the Lord." For that we thank God with all our hearts. You will also read that they were indeed very blessed and privileged to be the ones chosen by our Lord and our Lady of Combermere to be there. I need not say any more. I will let their beautiful and moving account speak for itself.

I'm sure most of my readers know that, during her lifetime, we simply called Catherine "B," and that is how our two dear sisters, Alma Coffman and Carol Ann Giske, refer to her. Alma is a nurse, Carol Ann is not. What I present here are excerpts from transcribed tape recordings, one made on the very day of Catherine's death, several others made at later dates. As the account begins, they are speaking about December 13–14.

Alma: Carol Ann Gieske and I were with B from the 11 P.M. to 7 A.M. shift. I was the "sleeper." That means the one who slept in a sleeping bag in the closet on the floor, ready at a moment's notice to give help with B to the one who stayed awake during the night.

About 12 midnight B was on her left side. As she became restless we turned her on her right side. She rested more quietly, although her respirations continued to be labored. During the night I encouraged Carol Ann to tell B that Fr. Eddie loved her and was waiting for her. B never talked during the night. Sometimes her respirations turned to groans. We turned her; it seemed quite uncomfortable for her to be turned—to move her arms and legs.

Carol Ann: When I came at 11:00 B's breathing was rather labored—more than the day before. She half-opened her eyes a few times during the night. She also made attempts to move her arm. Her breathing slowed down and she seemed to sleep for about an hour. I noticed when we turned her she seemed so stiff. I had a hard time positioning her, and asked Alma to do it at 4:00.

While preparing to turn her at 4:00 to her right side she reached up as she usually did to embrace me—to feel my warmth, as Archbishop Raya says. As she reached up, I moved down to embrace her. She would not have had the strength to hug me, but there we were, her arm across my back. So I hugged her, told her I loved her and our Lady loved her, and all the saints and angels loved her.

Sometime—I guess between 12 and 2:00—while her breathing was so heavy, I really sensed "here is a soul fighting to leave its body." Until recently B seemed to be fighting to stay, but no more. I prayed for mercy, prayed it would not have to be that often long dragged out process of dying. I prayed the Glorious Mysteries and half of the Joyful Mysteries.

Fr. Paul Bechard came in about 4:30 and stayed for a while, quietly praying; he blessed us all. He asked me how she was. Alma had lain down. I pointed out B's breathing. I asked if he had seen her yesterday. I didn't say what I thought. I really didn't expect her to die yet, since she had that restful period. What did I know! I couldn't tell Fr. Paul how she was. He left shortly before 5:00, I think.

Alma got up every two hours and was up for half the time at least. I was glad to be on with Alma and she with me. I mention it because the harmony between us was one of love and peace. So there was no tension in the atmosphere. Alma stayed at B's side while I cleaned the cabin after the 4:00 A.M. turning. I had just finished when Fr. Paul came in.

Alma: I slept in the closet a few times between turnings earlier in the night. Fr. Paul came in. But when I got up at 4 a.m. to give her her medicines, I wasn't tired. But at 5:10 a.m. I decided to lie down and relax. I wasn't sleepy. I started to pray for each member of the MH family by name when I heard Carol Ann say, in an urgent voice,

"Alma!" Instantly I was on my feet and out of the closet and beside B's bed.

She had her eyes closed and she was having a mild seizure. Her hands and arms were extended and trembling.

Carol Ann: She was breathing heavily as earlier in the night. It was about 5:20 when she gave a sudden loud gasp and stopped breathing. I called Alma. She came immediately to B's side. B's face was rigid, although she hadn't moved.

Alma asked me to ring Fr. Brière's bell, call Marian Heiberger and ask her and Jean Fox to come.

Alma: As the seizures stopped, B's respirations also stopped. She had a few very irregular breaths. Fr. Brière came in just as she gave the last big breath. After that there were several very shallow respirations; then that was all. We did get out the suction machine, but we never used it, or the oxygen. It was all over so quick. And there was a deep sense of peace.

I said to Carol Ann, "This is a great moment!" There B lay—no struggle, no pain. She was free at last. It was 5:30 a.m. Fr. Brière gives her the Last Communion and blessing. At some point Fr. Brière takes her in his arms and kneels beside the bed.

Marian Heiberger comes in, and then Elizabeth Bassarear, Jean Fox, Mary Davis, Jim Guinan. Fr. Brière asked me to lead the rosary. I started with the Apostles' Creed, but got mixed up with it and went on to the Hail Marys. Fr. Brière starts the prayers for the dead. Fr. Bob Pelton arrives as does B's son George and members of the MH family. There is a reverent coming and going. Sandra Wood from the R.A. sobs. Angela Redmond sings a solo, "Regina" in English—beautiful! Jean Fox says, "Catherine of Combermere, pray for us." The applicants come. Then around 6:25 Fr. Brière has Mass.

Alma and Carol Ann recorded the following a few days later, on December 19:

Alma: Do you remember I said, "Carol Ann, this is one of the most important moments of our life."? Is that what I said?

Carol Ann: Well, I think it is. I remember that you came over and put your arm around my shoulder like you sometimes did when we were working together, and you said, "Carol Ann, this is one of the most important moments in our lives." We knew it was really important.

Alma: You know it was really a privilege. We both had just worked together in the herb garden, and you had just taken first promises on the 8th. I had taken first promises in '81. So this made me four years into promises. So we both were young in the apostolate. But here we were with this great privilege of being with the foundress when she died. And it wasn't a privilege that anyone could ask for. And I had been praying for everyone by name. It wasn't something that I could have orchestrated or known, but just the guiding of the Spirit. It was like we were standing there for the whole MH family, both the present ones and those who would ever wear the pax-caritas cross. It was just a beautiful moment.

It was a scary moment, too, in some ways. But there was a tremendous peace there, but also to decide what did we need to do. Was this really the moment of B's death or was this just a seizure, which she had had before? Would this be something that when she came out of it she was going to need oxygen? Was she going to need suctioning? You know, so we were intent on getting the things ready; but at the same time we were attentive to her at the moment of her death, so it had a lot of mixed emotions with it. Also, what was coming from B was peace.

Carol Ann: It was interesting. At one of the wakes Fr. Wild said, "What happened is, Jesus came and kissed her and took her home." And to me that so describes how B did die, because she gave a big gasp. It was a gasp. She had been breathing a labored breathing. I'm not a nurse, and haven't seen—she's only the second person that I saw die. So I'm not actually up on exactly what happened. But I thought that B died at that point. So I called Alma; I called you right away. It was like the Lord came and kissed her and took her home. It happened very quickly.

Now people want to know or ask, "Did you smell any flowers? Did you see anything unusual like lights? Did you hear any bells ringing?" I did not. But maybe Alma has something to add.

Alma: It was a very ordinary death in the sense that you had a person who was breathing in a dying rhythm, but there was a deep sense of peace. I would say that B's spirit quietly left her body. Very, very quietly. There was no thrashing, really no struggle, at the moment of her death. Her breathing just went into what I would call a dying rhythm—a few big breaths, a few short breaths, a big breath, a short breath, a lessening of intervals between the breaths, and then, at last no breath.

And you know what I see as the biggest miracle of B's life and death? It's not anything that happened, but the fact that we have vocations to Madonna House and that we can persevere in them. That, to me, is the biggest sign of B's holiness, is that all of us have been called to this vocation.

Alma: We buried Catherine Doherty yesterday, December 18, Wednesday. I buried my foundress. I buried the only living person I'd ever met who had a vision of God and how to live the gospel big enough for me to leave everything and to follow what she lived and saw. Prior to my first contact with Madonna House, I had been nurtured and loved deeply and beautifully by many people. But never did I meet God in such a profound vision that I needed to leave family, friends, homeland, church, all my possessions, and follow after that which my heart longed for; and that is God in the Absolute; to preach the gospel with my life without compromise, according to the spirit of Madonna House.

Death is a Bridge

Catherine's reflections on the death of Fr. Eddie, May 6, 1975, and July 28, 1976:

All of us realize that death is a bridge. It seems that all the psychiatrists and psychologists are telling us that we fear death. This is why we are filling ourselves with pills and this, that and the other thing. Death and pain are the two things we want to eschew. And yet, in the person of Fr. Eddie, man realizes that death is a bridge, a most wonderful bridge that you have to cross in order to find, not only peace and love, but God himself.

There is nothing to be afraid of. Rather than fear, death brings out a fantastic feeling of expectation that is like a man or woman waiting for their date. So we Christians should wait for our *date*—the immense, fantastic, incredible, explosive, joyful, peaceful encounter with God. For it is a date. For this we have been born—that we should be one with the Lord.

Death is a bridge that you begin to walk when you are very small that ends in the arms of God. It is so very, very simple. This bridge is, in a sense, the essence of the Good News. He came to give us life everlasting. He died so that we could say, "Death, where is your sting?" He conquered death for us. Do we believe that?

We have to face the ultimate essence of our fear. We have to enter the realm of faith. I happened to enter into it last year. Eddie died on May 4, and my very favorite brother, Serge, died on May 20th. Now, what is death? I think I shocked a lot of people in our Russian chapel by dancing around Eddie's coffin. How was I able to dance? Because God in his infinite mercy has given me faith.

Suppose that your husband, your best friend, your wife, your boy friend, your girl friend, died. If you really loved that person with a true love, shouldn't you be delighted? Shouldn't you be excited? Wouldn't you be sort of dancing in your heart that he or she is going to see God? Can you imagine—*the one you loved is seeing God face to face!*

Why don't we enter into the wonderful theological virtue of hope and say to ourselves: "God is so merciful. Why do I go around fearing death? I am filled with the hope of the hereafter, of seeing God, of being with him. Don't let me be afraid of death. Let me welcome it like St. Francis welcomed 'Sister Death.' Welcome her with open arms. Because, as I stretch out my hand towards Sister Death, I meet the wounded hands of Christ. I am embraced by him, and he kisses me with the kiss of his mouth, as it says in the Canticle of Canticles. I think that is what is going to happen when I die: suddenly he will kiss me with the kiss of his mouth.

Let us drop the fear of death, because in that fear, hidden like a sort of fungus, are a thousand other fears that would disappear if we stopped being afraid of death. I don't know if that makes any impression on you, but I really mean it. Death, my friends, is fun!

Death is a bridge over which we have to pass, but it is so nice to prepare oneself to walk over a bridge. Even though there are lots of precipices, lots of surging waters beneath the bridge, faith will take us across, love will give us the strength to help someone else across, and hope will make a song our of life.

So let us be in peace, in joy, in gladness that Fr. Doherty has passed over the bridge, and that he and the High Priest, the real Priest, Christ, have now met. So let us praise the Lord! Come on, let us sing an Alleluia! (Everyone sings Alleluia!)

The Beauty and Glory of Her Death

Excerpts from various homilies at services after Catherine's death:

Today, this morning, all the loneliness of all the people she had ever met, her own loneliness, all the sinfulness, all the hurt, everything was pushed away, and today Jesus kissed her without anything in between. That's what happened today. Who can imagine what that is, the explosion of his hidden presence! For all those years Jesus veiled himself from her, in us, in the poor, hiding himself, and her seeking him. But today, the veil was removed, and Jesus kissed her with the kiss of his mouth. That's what happened today. —*Fr. Bob Wild*

In her mind, in her understanding of God's call, it is that element of personal transformation, of making a community of love, that is the work of Madonna House, and the means by which the vocation of the apostolate will be accomplished. Unless the grain of wheat falls to the earth and dies, it only remains a single grain. And as we see, Catherine has fallen to the earth and died over and over and over again in her life, and has brought forth a rich harvest. And again this moment in which she again falls to the earth and dies hold in it a promise for a rich harvest, not only for us but for the whole world. —*Fr. Bob Sharkey*

Let us rejoice then tonight. We have seen what so many prophets and kings yearned to see. How many Benedictines would have loved to know St. Benedict? How many tens of thousands of Franciscans would have given anything if they could have just met Francis once?

And yet, God has selected us to know and to live with, these precious years, our foundress and our mother. So tonight we look to the heart of the Trinity where B is dancing and laughing and singing as she promised she would with her golden slippers. And we on earth celebrate too, by pointing not to B, but pointing to Jesus Christ who leads each one of us to the heart of the Father, the fullness of love of the Spirit, and always in the heart of Mary, the Mother of God. —*Fr. Jim Duffy*

But as Catherine became littler and littler, weaker, more helpless, the glory of her life became brighter. She had asked the Lord what she could give, what she could give in love to him, what she could give in praise of him, what she could give to feed the hungry, to heal the sick, what she could give for the Church, what she could give for priests and Sisters, what she could give for Madonna House, what she could give for the thousands of people who wrote to her or knew of her. And he said to her, "Your life." And she said, "Well, I sing and sing because I give you such a small thing." But she couldn't have known, really, that it was going to be poured out for the last eighteen months, drop by drop.

My brothers and sisters, if we can see the beauty and the glory of this death, we can see the Lord whom Catherine loved so much and who loved her so much. Because truly, no matter how unusual were all the circumstances surrounding her death—not everyone has a community like Madonna House to care for them when they're old; not everyone has the incredible physique and genetic inheritance and the grace and so forth to live what Catherine lived; not everyone can be so surrounded by prayer and holiness—nevertheless, her death was very ordinary. There are thousands of old people at home or in nursing homes who die in this slow, passing way. Catherine became a poor woman. Obviously, not an ordinary one: here we all are. But she became a poor woman.

And in that total abandonment of herself to Jesus Christ, we see his compassion and his presence to every single person who lives and who breathes.

For years, people have been saying, "What will happen when Catherine dies?" I think the thing we never thought of really clearly—some perhaps did—was, well, when Catherine dies, she's going to see Jesus Christ; she's going to be in the arms of the Lord; she's going to live in the heart of the Blessed Trinity. Will she grow less? No. Now is the time for her to grow great. What will happen when Catherine dies? The seed that she allowed the Lord to make of her has been planted so deep in the earth of this world and in the light of eternity that it will continue to grow and send out roots and send up branches, and it will stretch across the face of the earth. And the words that she has spoken will be read as long as men and women read English, or read any other language, for that matter. And the family that God has taken from her flesh, from her spirit, will become—if only our friends pray for us, and if only we do the little things exceedingly well for the love of God—will become a unity of faith and love that will be a bright star in the sky for as long as the Lord wants it to shine.

May we give glory to him who has loved us so much by giving us so great, so holy, so joyful, so wise, and so childlike a woman. Thank you. Thank you, Catherine. Thank you, Blessed Mother of God, Our Lady of Combermere. Thank you, Father, Son and Holy Spirit. May you be praised in Catherine and in all of us her children, now and always and forever and ever. —*Fr. Bob Pelton, Homily at Catherine's Resurrection Mass, December 18, 1985.*

The Habit and the Slippers

It was said that when Catherine knew she was dying, she exacted a promise from the members of the community at Madonna House that when her body was placed in the coffin, it was to be attired in her Third Order Franciscan Habit (yes, she was one of us!) and her dancing slippers were to be put on her feet. The reason for this Habit was obvious, but "Why the dancing slippers, B?" "Because when I get there, I'm going to spend eternity dancing with the Holy and Blessed Trinity."

When Catherine died a few days later, her body was placed in a coffin which was hand-made from a few planks sawn from a great, white pine felled on the grounds of Madonna House; and yes, she was attired in her Third Order Habit and her dancing slippers!" —*Brother Cuthbert, T.O.S., Sturgeon Falls, Ontario*

Final Word

One final tidbit from the internet that cheered up this postulator, and put him in goodly company. Speaking about those working on a cause: "Above all, it requires faith, for scant few of those who dedicate their lives to a candidate will live to see whether the cause succeeds, or [if his cause] becomes one of 'the silent ones', the causes on behalf of people whose applications for sainthood end up languishing forever in the Vatican's musty archives."

The Holy Spirit is the Chief Postulator of all the causes, Catherine's as well. Catherine, and her spiritual legacy, belong to the Church. We are seeking to discover God's will as regards her being raised to the altar for the edification of God's people. It's certainly true that not all holy people are canonized, especially when you consider the "great multitude" described in Revelations (19:1). Pray, dear reader, that God's will be done in regards to Catherine. I think it's a legitimate prayer to ask God to please let her be canonized. At least, that's how I pray!

Endnotes

1. Trans. Joseph Daries, C.M.F. Claret Center for Resources in Spirituality, Religious Life Series, Vol. 5 (Chicago, Los Angeles, Manila). 1983.

2. Cf. Lorene Hanley Duquin, *They Called Her the Baroness*. (Alba House, New York, 1995).

3. All of Catherine's books (and a free catalogue) can be obtained from our center in Canada: Madonna House, 2888 Dafoe Rd, Combermere ON, K0J 1L0 — or on-line at: http://www.madonnahouse.org/publications/

4. I was the director of our program for a number of years. See my book *Chambers of Her Heart: Madonna House and Priestly Formation* (Madonna House Publications).

Catherine Doherty–
Biographical Milestones

1896
On August 15, Catherine is born in a Pullman car, during the great fair of Nijni-Novgorod, in Russia. Daughter of Theodore and Emma Kolyschkine, minor nobles. Baptized according to Orthodox ritual in Saint Petersburg.

1903–1909
Student at the convent school of the Sisters of Our Lady of Zion, a Roman Catholic order, in Ramleh, Eygpt.

1912
Catherine's marriage to her first cousin Boris de Hueck, celebrated in the Orthodox cathedral of Saint Isaac in Saint Petersburg.

1913–1917
First World War and the Bolshevik revolution. Catherine is a nurse stationed on the front lines, and is decorated for bravery.

1918
Boris and Catherine are condemned to death by starvation, by Finnish communists, at their summer home, Merri-Lokki, in Finland. Catherine promises God to consecrate her life to him if he will rescue her.

1919
Escape to England. Catherine joins the Roman Catholic Church during a celebration held on December 31.

1921
Catherine moves to Toronto with Boris; birth of their son George on July 17.

1922–1929

Life of a refugee. In the beginning, poorly paid small jobs. Then the period of well paid lectures. Catherine remembers her promise. Uneasiness. In 1924 joins the Third Order Franciscans through the Gray Friars of the Atonement, founded by Paul Watson at Graymoor; remains a member until her death.

1930–1933

Separation from Boris. Student nurse in Montreal. In 1931 Catherine does a private survey of the inroads of Communism in Toronto at the request of Archbishop Neil McNeil of Toronto. Helps other immigrants.

1934–1936

Opens Friendship House in Toronto.

1937

As a journalist, Catherine covers the Spanish Civil War and also the Communist expansion, and the spread of Catholic Action, in France and Belgium.

1938

On February 14 she settles in New York and opens a Friendship House in the slums of Harlem. Also lectures all across the United States for interracial justice; is on the cutting edge of the Civil Rights movement.

1939

Sojourn in Europe for the compilation of a series of articles on the comportment of Catholics in face of the rise of Nazism. Catherine in Poland on September 1, during the bombardment and invasion of that country by Hitler.

1942

Opens a Friendship House in the slums of Chicago.

1943

Annulment of her marriage to Boris de Hueck. Marriage with Eddie Doherty, Chicago reporter, by the auxillary bishop of Chicago, Bishop Bernard Sheil.

1946

The members of Friendship House split over Catherine's vision and leadership.

1947

Together with her husband, Eddie, settles in Combermere, Ontario, on May 17.

1949

Beginning of the Summer School and the family apostolate in Combermere.

1950

In November, 1950, Catherine asks Fr. John Callahan to become her spiritual director and six months later he accepts. He later becomes the first priest to join Madonna House.

1951

On February 2, 1951, Catherine and Eddie consecrate themselves to Jesus through Mary according to the true devotion of St. Louis de Montfort. On October 15, 1951, Catherine has an audience with Pope Pius XII. Madonna House begins movement towards Secular Institute status.

1952

Catherine and Eddie consecrate themselves as victim souls for priests.

1955–1959

On October 30, 1955, Eddie and Catherine make their vow of chastity (celibacy). Cana Colony, a summer camp for families, is opened. St. Benedict's Acres, the Madonna House farm, is begun.

1960

The statue of Our Lady of Combermere is blessed by Bishop Smith on June 8.

1961–1969

Catherine writes several books on the origins of her apostolate and on different aspects of her spirituality. May 31, 1963: the ordination of the first priest for Madonna House, Fr. Robert Pelton. In 1966 Vianney House, a house for priests, is opened. In 1969 Eddie is ordained a Melkite Catholic priest.

1970–1985

Catherine continues to write, notably her "Madonna House Classics" and other works. On May 4, 1975 Eddie dies. On March 14, 1980 Catherine has audience with Pope John Paul II. Catherine dies on December 14, 1985, following four years of health problems and their attendant extreme suffering; she makes the gift of her life, cell by cell.

2000

Fr. Wild is appointed postulator, and the process is begun towards the opening of Catherine's cause for canonization. At the time Madonna House had 200 members in 20 countries, and 100 Associate Priests.

More information about Catherine Doherty
and her cause for canonization:

www.catherinedoherty.org

Information about the Madonna House Apostolate:

www.madonnahouse.org

Books by Catherine Doherty and Fr. Wild:

www.madonnahouse.org/publications

To contact the postulator for the cause, write to:

Postulator
Madonna House Apostolate
2888 Dafoe Rd
Combermere ON K0J 1L0

or e-mail:

postulator@catherinedoherty.org

We welcome donations to help cover cause expenses.

Fr. Wild also has a personal web site
featuring some of his books and articles:

www.fatherbobwild.org.uk